Library of
Davidson College

Foreign Investment in the U.S.: Costs and Benefits

by Elliot Zupnick

CONTENTS

	Foreword *by Raymond Vernon*	3
1	The Open Investment System Challenged	6
2	The Why and How of Direct Investment	12
3	Direct Investment: A Statistical Portrait	34
4	Banking: A Special Case	51
5	What Future for Open Investment?	71
	Statistical tables on pp. 35, 36, 40, 41, 42, 44, 46, 48, 57, 65	
	Glossary	76
	Talking It Over	78

HEADLINE Series 249, April 1980 $2.00

Cover by: Design Works

The Author

ELLIOT ZUPNICK is professor of International Economics at Columbia University. He previously taught at C.C.N.Y., The City University Graduate School and Cornell University. He is the author of numerous books and articles on international economics, including two previous HEADLINE Series: "Primer on United States Foreign Economic Policy" (169) and "Understanding the International Monetary System" (182).

The Foreign Policy Association

The Foreign Policy Association is a private, nonprofit, nonpartisan educational organization. Its purpose is to stimulate wider interest and more effective participation in, and greater understanding of, world affairs among American citizens. Among its activities is the continuous publication, dating from 1935, of the HEADLINE Series pamphlets. The authors of these pamphlets are responsible for factual accuracy and for the views expressed. FPA itself takes no position on issues of United States foreign policy.

Editorial Advisory Committee
Hans J. Morgenthau, *chairman*

W. Phillips Davison
John Lewis Gaddis
Keith Goldhammer
Antonie T. Knoppers

William H. McNeill
Edwin Newman
Stanley E. Spangler
Richard H. Ullman

The HEADLINE Series (ISSN 0017-8780) is published February, April, August, October and December by the Foreign Policy Association, Inc., 205 Lexington Ave., New York, N.Y. 10016. Chairman, Carter L. Burgess; Editor, Wallace Irwin, Jr.; Associate Editor, Gwen Crowe. Subscription rates, $8.00 for 5 issues; $15.00 for 10 issues; $21.00 for 15 issues. Single copy price $2.00. Discount 25% on 10 to 99 copies; 30% on 100 to 499; 35% on 500 to 999; 40% on 1,000 or more. Payment must accompany order for $5 or less. Second-class postage paid at New York, N.Y. Copyright 1980 by Foreign Policy Association, Inc. Composed and printed at Science Press, Ephrata, Penn.

Library of Congress Catalog No. 80-66684
ISBN 0-87124-061-0

Foreword

by Raymond Vernon

Some of us are old enough to remember Orson Welles' great radio spoof one Saturday night 40 years ago, when he played anchorman in a one-hour program covering the invasion of a fleet of belligerent Martian spaceships. Many listeners tuned in late, missing the opening commercials. In no time at all the roads out of New York, Washington and Philadelphia were jammed with the motor chariots of millions of doughty Americans fleeing for the high country.

The Martians, some appear to think, are with us again—this time in the form of a few hundred firms from Canada, Europe and Japan that have set up shop on American soil. In this case, it is true, their belligerence is carefully disguised. Indeed, all they appear to be doing is offering to hire American labor to produce their goods on American soil.

For decades, our own U.S. firms have been penetrating the economies of foreign countries on a vastly larger scale. One-half of Canada's industry, one-quarter of Mexico's industry, one-tenth of Europe's industry are made up of the subsidiaries of American firms. For many years, the economies of Jamaica, Venezuela, and dozens of other countries rose and fell on the production and exports of a few American enterprises operating in their economies. When from time to time the governments of these countries were misguided enough to worry about their exposed position, we were quick enough to put them right. The operation of our free enterprise system, we patiently explained, would generate jobs and increase productivity, a return easily worth the price of a little exposure to foreigners.

If I were to assert that the shoe is on the other foot today, I

Raymond Vernon is Clarence Dillon Professor of International Affairs at Harvard University's Center for International Affairs. He is author of many books including *Storm Over the Multinationals: The Real Issues* (1977) and *Sovereignty at Bay: The Multinational Spread of U.S. Enterprises* (1971).

would be grossly distorting the facts. The direct investments of foreigners in the United States amount to scarcely more than a shoestring, certainly not to a shoe; such investments come to less than 5 percent of our country's corporate assets, hardly enough to be visible.

To shut off serious discussion of the implications of foreign direct investment in the United States, however, would be a mistake. Like Professor Zupnick, I foresee a good deal more of such investment over the coming years. Unlike him, I am not altogether sure that the consequences of such increased investment will all be favorable. But at the present stage, the case for restriction simply does not exist.

In some respects, the direct investments of foreigners represent an anomaly in international relations. We have carved up our earth space into separate national territories and we have charged the governments of each territory to ensure peace, security and prosperity in their respective domains. Then, almost as an afterthought, we have arranged to allow the enterprises that make the goods and deliver the services on which these governments rely to spread themselves all over the globe. The result: From an economic point of view, governments cannot even pretend to be in charge of the economies over which they are elected to preside.

The case for continuing to live with the absurd system we have created is the case that Winston Churchill once made for democracy. What we now have doesn't work very well; but any regime that would separate our economy from the others by restricting foreign investment would be a great deal worse. To be sure, persistent changes in the modern technology of transportation and communication have been entangling every country in the arms and legs of every other. But at this stage, it is fatuous to talk of disengaging ourselves; our capital markets, our monetary systems, our technological networks, and our raw material positions are inextricably intertwined.

What to do? Certainly not to pretend that all is well in the best of all serendipitous worlds. There are problems and contradictions galore in the peculiar international system that we have so far absentmindedly created. There are conflicts of national jurisdiction as in banking, antitrust, pollution and foreign investment; these promise real trouble ahead. And there are gaps in national jurisdiction that may prove just as troublesome, as in the deep sea and outer space. But none of these problems can be dealt with constructively by any single nation. Professor Zupnick's admonition that we will be cutting off our collective noses if we try to deal with the problems of foreign direct investments by unilateral action is a warning to be heeded. Like other problems of this type, its amelioration demands the scarcest of all ingredients in international affairs, namely, a cooperative approach among nations.

Everyone will have his or her own estimate as to whether such an approach will be forthcoming. It is easy to be cynical on that score; but the cynic is often wrong. Some remarkable international institutions have been created in the past 20 years or so to deal with the unprecedented problems of international economic policy, institutions that would have been inconceivable in another era. These range from a widespread network of highly technical treaties that now reconcile the conflicting tax laws of different countries, to an informal club among the world's leading central bankers that now meets monthly on neutral Swiss territory. If only such institutions could be made to evolve as rapidly as the problems they confront, we might all be home free. In the field of foreign direct investment, however, the development of the problems has so far been outdistancing the institutions for dealing with them. In any constructive solution to the problems that go with foreign direct investment, the size of that gap will have to be greatly reduced.

1
The Open Investment System Challenged

In 1978 Kenneth C. Crowe wrote a book entitled *America for Sale*. His basic message was that foreign investments in the United States have already reached a level where they represent a clear and present danger. These investments, he wrote, have not only enabled foreigners to secure control over important and sensitive sectors of the American economy; they have also given foreigners inordinate influence over American foreign policies. The Arab investors' potential impact on American policies toward Israel was prominently cited as a case in point.

Crowe's is not a lonely voice in the wilderness. For the past few years, the news media have highlighted the expansion of foreign investments in the United States and the threat that this is felt to represent. Foreign expansion in the banking industry, with particular emphasis on the acquisition of large American banks, has been widely publicized. In late 1979 the CBS television program "Sixty Minutes" devoted a segment to anxious reports that Arab investors and others, perhaps with sinister motives, were buying up large blocks of American farmland. Soon afterward, *Newsweek* ran a cover story to much the same effect.

The article implied, if it did not actually state, that the United States was threatened with the loss of its most precious resource. Readers of realty news have been made aware of foreign investments in America's great cities; for example, a German bank's interest in acquiring New York's twin World Trade Towers, until recently the tallest buildings in the world, was featured prominently in the national press.

The increased activities of foreign investors have not passed unnoticed in Washington. In November 1979, the Senate approved a measure to impose a six-month moratorium on foreign acquisitions of American banks. Previous congressional acts directed various governmental agencies to collect and disseminate data on foreign investments. While the declared objective of this legislation was merely informational, there is no doubt that it was motivated, in part, by a desire to monitor foreign investments and, if necessary, to restrict them.

The U.S. Policy and Its Critics

If this implied threat of restriction of foreign investment were carried out, the result would be a basic change in U.S. official policy in this area. The present American policy was briefly summarized by Charles F. Meissner, Deputy Assistant Secretary for International Finance and Development of the Department of State at a hearing before a subcommittee of the Committee on Foreign Affairs in 1979: "The United States," he stated, "has long believed that flows of trade, finance and investment can make their most effective contribution to long term, steady economic growth in an open climate in which these flows can respond to market forces. *Consistent with our belief in such an open system, general U.S. international investment policy is not to adopt government measures which either promote or discourage inward or outward investment flows. We favor a system which offers the same opportunities to both foreign and domestic investors on a nondiscriminatory basis.* [Italics supplied.] We believe such a system will engender increased overall direct investment flows which are particularly important today to many countries, both in the developed and developing world. Among the benefits of such increased direct investment flows are more jobs, more capital, transfers of new, improved technology and management skills, increased production, and greater competition."

Direct Investme

*Simply defined, a **foreign direct investment**, or FDI (sometimes just called direct investment, the word "foreign" being understood) is a business enterprise located in one country but controlled in another. The control is exercised through total or partial ownership of the stock in the enterprise, usually by a "parent" company.*

Direct investment is not the only kind. Most foreign investment, in fact, is portfolio *investment, in which the investor either lends money to a foreign government or business, or buys a less-than-controlling share of stock in a business enterprise. The purpose of portfolio investment is chiefly to get a return in the form of interest, dividends or capital gains rather than to control or influence company or governmental policy. Any individual who owns a bond or a few shares of stock in a business enterprise is a portfolio investor. Insurance companies, mutual funds, banks, universities and other institutions are portfolio investors on a much larger scale.*

The present study, however, deals only with direct investments that involve foreign control.

Control of an enterprise normally rests with whoever owns the largest single block of shares of its voting stock. Ownership of more than 50 percent of a company stock automatically confers control, since the votes of a majority of shares can elect the board of directors and determine company policy. Often, however, where a company's stock is dispersed among many stockholders, effective control can be gained through ownership of quite a small percentage. As an extreme case, it has been estimated that whoever acquires a mere 2 percent of the stock of the huge

The basic premise of the existing U.S. policy, then, is that of an open international investment system in which governments treat domestic and foreign-owned enterprises exactly alike in accordance with the principle of nondiscrimination or "national

hat It Is

American Telephone and Telegraph Company, whose stock is dispersed among more than 3 million small shareholders, could control the company. Thus it is impossible to say with precision, based solely on percentage of share ownership, whether a given investment is sufficient to confer control. The U.S. Department of Commerce arbitrarily defines a "foreign direct investment" as a foreign equity in an enterprise amounting to at least 10 percent. There is no magic in that percentage; in a particular case 10 percent may be less or more than enough to confer control.

Control can be gained by purchase of some or all of an existing company's stock, either on the open market or, more often, by negotiation. This type of transaction is called an acquisition. *Alternatively, a firm wishing to embark on a new venture may invest in an entirely new subsidiary company, either alone or as a joint venture with other owners in which it holds the controlling share.*

A final note on how a direct investment "position" is measured. The standard measure is the book value of the stock owned by the parent company, plus or minus the net value of loans outstanding between the parent and its affiliate. This, however, may understate the degree of control exercised by foreigners. Where the foreign parent company's equity is less than 100 percent, the value of the enterprise it controls is greater than its actual share. Thus, although the total value of FDIs in the United States in 1978 was listed at $41 billion, the value of foreign-controlled enterprises was considerably greater. And by the same token, the value of U.S.-controlled enterprises abroad in the same year was considerably greater than the official $168 billion total.

treatment." Critics of the policy directly challenge this philosophy. They argue, among other things, that the United States is virtually alone in adhering to an "open door" policy, and in this they are not entirely wrong. Most less-developed countries (LDCs), for example, not only require governmental approval for new foreign investments but increasingly attach conditions to those investments which they do approve. Thus many LDCs have enacted "indigenization" laws which require foreign companies operating under their jurisdictions to reserve specified proportions of job categories for the indigenous populations. Other laws provide for increased sharing of technology, reinvestment of some minimum percentage of earnings, host country equity in joint ventures with foreign enterprises and even the gradual phasing out of foreign ownership.

This tendency to impose conditions on foreign investments is not limited, moreover, to the less-developed countries. Almost all Western European governments have screening procedures to ensure that incoming foreign investments promote their national objectives, and many have placed some sectors of their economy off limits for foreign investors. Few, if any, Western European countries, for example, permit foreigners to purchase farmland or to acquire existing banks. Japan is even more restrictive. The low level of foreign direct investments (FDIs) in that country speaks eloquently to its success in keeping foreign firms out. Thus, although the Japanese economy is approximately 40 percent the size of the European Economic Community (EEC), the American investment position in Japan is but 9 percent of that in the EEC. In fact, the value of American direct investments in Japan is less than its direct investments in Switzerland, Australia and Brazil.

Critics of the present American investment policy argue that adherence to an open investment system in the face of these restrictions puts U.S. firms at a competitive disadvantage. If foreigners wish to enjoy the freedom to invest in the United States, they should be prepared to extend full reciprocity to American investors. Failing this, it is argued, the United States, on economic grounds, should impose comparable restrictions on foreign investors. These economic arguments are reinforced by those of other critics who believe that for security and other noneconomic reasons the United States should modify its present policies regarding FDIs.

The primary objective of this essay is to determine whether a restrictive U.S. policy as it relates to foreign direct investment in the United States is desirable. Chapter 2 analyzes the factors affecting FDIs and examines the costs and benefits of these investments. Chapter 3 presents a "statistical portrait" and evaluation of the FDI position in the United States. Chapter 4 contains a detailed case study of the FDI position in the "sensitive" banking industry. Chapter 5 explores the reasons behind the drive to restrict FDIs and summarizes the conclusions drawn from this study.

2
The Why and How of Direct Investment

Foreign direct investment is not a new phenomenon. Students of history are aware of the crucial role played by the East India Company in the British conquest of India and of the activities of the various "charter" companies in the settlement and colonization of the Americas, Africa and Asia. It was not until recent times, however, that FDI became a dominant feature of the world economy. The major reason for this is the spectacular growth, in the aftermath of World War II, of the multinational enterprise. American corporations have been in the vanguard of this movement. Even today, they account for more than half of the world total of direct investments.

As already noted, the major focus of this essay is on FDIs in the United States. The present interest in these investments is due not to their being a new phenomenon, but rather to the fact that only in the 1970s did the United States become a *major* target country for foreign investors. It is important to bear in mind, however, that even the present increased level of foreign investments in this country constitutes a small fraction of the world total. Their recent growth pattern, moreover, far from being *sui generis*, reflects the same forces that earlier induced American corporations, on a much vaster scale, to invest abroad.

This global context has important implications. Among other things, it permits us to draw upon the total post-World War II experience, both here and abroad, to make a *general* analysis of FDIs. In this way we shall analyze the factors responsible for their growth, the benefits derived from them by both the investors and the host countries, and the problems, real and imagined, which they pose for the host countries. The insights derived from this analysis should stand us in good stead when attention is turned to the primary problem of this study: an appraisal of the desirability of altering American foreign investment policy.

The first part of this chapter, then, is devoted to an analysis of the major factors that have induced companies, of whatever nationality, to make FDIs on an increasing scale. The second part reviews the costs and benefits of these investments to the host countries, and touches on the policies of host country governments in this connection.

Why Companies 'Go Abroad'

The dramatic growth of multinational enterprises in the postwar period has transformed them into major actors in the world economy. In this role, they have been both praised and denounced. To their admirers, they are the most important engines of growth ever devised by human ingenuity. Their detractors, on the other hand, view them as the cutting edge of neocolonialism and neo-imperialism. They have been hailed as economic liberators and denounced as exploiters. The one fate they have avoided is that of being ignored; few subjects have received more attention in international forums in recent years than the multinational enterprise.

Whatever its ultimate impact on the economies and societies of the host countries, whether as a benefactor or as an exploiter, the *pursuit of profits is normally the principal fundamental purpose behind a firm's decision to invest abroad.* A firm goes abroad to attain one or more of several specific objectives involved in its effort to maximize profits. The most frequent of these objectives are to obtain from the host country a secure and stable supply of those raw materials on which its operations depend; to manufacture at reduced cost in the host country with a view to exporting to other countries, improving its competitive position in their markets; and to sell more effectively in the host country's own market.

These objectives not only explain *why* a firm invests abroad; they also determine in large measure *where* it invests. If, for example, the objective is to secure its raw materials, its options are constrained by the facts of geography and geology. The Aluminum Company of America's large investments in bauxite-rich Jamaica, the Kennecott Copper Company's large investments in Chile, and the long-dominant investment position of the "seven sisters," the world's leading oil companies, in the Middle East, all illustrate this point.

If, on the other hand, a firm's objective is to reduce its manufacturing costs in order to improve its competitive position on the world market, the choice of where to invest is determined by the nature of its product and by how well the prospective host countries are endowed with the *factors of production* (land, raw materials, labor, etc.) most appropriate to that product. A firm producing labor-intensive products will seek out host countries that have dependable, intelligent labor forces willing to work for relatively low wage rates. American, European and Japanese producers of clothing, textiles, footwear, consumer electronics and other labor-intensive goods have for this reason invested heavily in, among other places, Taiwan, South Korea, Singapore and Hong Kong. These newly industrializing countries (NICs), as they have come to be called, have, in effect, become "export platforms" for the multinational corporations (MNCs). This type of foreign investment has been severely criticized by the labor unions in the more advanced countries on the ground that it is tantamount to an export of jobs. The MNCs' response to this criticism is that were they to attempt to produce labor-intensive goods using high-wage labor they could not remain competitive.

With some exceptions—foreign investment in the American petroleum industry being the chief one—the first two objectives played a minor role in inducing FDIs in the United States. The reason for this is not hard to find. The United States is neither a low-cost producing country nor is it a country on which others rely for their basic raw materials. Indeed, the vast majority of foreign investors motivated by the desire to secure a steady supply of raw materials or by the need to reduce manufacturing costs are located in the LDCs.

The principal reason foreign corporations establish branches in the United States, and for that matter why American corporations establish branches in Western Europe and Canada, is to produce goods and services for sale in the host countries' affluent markets. This is clearly reflected in Department of Commerce data which show the destination of sales by majority-owned foreign affiliates of United States corporations. In 1976 the total sales of these affiliates amounted to $515 billion, of which 65 percent went to the host country markets, 27 percent to third-country markets and 7 percent to the American markets. (It is interesting to note that the sales to the American markets consisted, in roughly equal parts, of petroleum and manufactured goods.) While similar data for foreign affiliates operating in the United States are not available, it is almost certain that these affiliates sell an even higher proportion of their goods in the American markets than U.S. affiliates operating abroad sell in the host country markets.

A Key Choice: Export or Invest?

This dominant objective of the direct investor—the desire to penetrate the host countries' markets—would seem at first glance to require no explanation. In fact, however, it poses some important conceptual problems which must be clarified if the recent growth of FDIs in this country is to be understood. The principal difficulty arises from the necessity to explain why foreign firms should even attempt to gain, or expand, a foothold in these markets by establishing subsidiaries when it would seem they could accomplish the same objective more easily through exports.* Firms operating in a foreign environment invariably incur costs that the local firms, with whom they are in competition, can avoid. These costs may be due to higher expenses for communication or transportation or, more generally, to the fact that foreign firms tend to have a less perfect knowledge of local markets and conditions. It would seem that these additional costs would surely weigh heavily against a decision to penetrate a foreign market by establishing subsidiaries within it and would encourage firms to place reliance on exports.

M.I.T. economist Charles Kindleberger, who was the first to pose this problem, suggested that a firm would not, in fact, set up foreign operations unless it had some more than offsetting advantages: superior technology, superior management, access to cheaper sources of supply or financing, a superior distribution system or the possession of a prestigious brand name that enables it to charge a higher price for its products and still remain competitive.

This explanation, however, only suggests the conditions that have to be satisfied before firms will even consider establishing foreign subsidiaries; it provides no guidance as to when they will actually do so. A general solution to this problem is, however, ready at hand. The key is that *a firm faced with a decision between exports and FDIs will choose the less costly method to attain its objective.* This decision, like most others in business, is made at the margin. The question is rarely an either/or choice

---

*There is, however, a third alternative which, while not explored in this essay, should be briefly noted. A firm may grant to foreign firms the right to use its patented technology for the production of goods abroad. This right, or license, is granted against payment of fees by the licensees to the licensor. Licensing has become an important avenue for the international diffusion of technology. It is a method frequently preferred by the licensee's government because it obviates the need for a foreign presence while assuring the local industry the benefits of modern technology. The attractiveness of this alternative to the licensing companies depends on the particular circumstances. Sometimes a firm will choose this route because it is unable or unwilling to export its products or to establish foreign subsidiaries. In other cases, the decision to license is made after a calculation of costs and potential revenues suggests that licensing is more profitable than exporting or FDIs.

between exports and an FDI. It is usually a question of whether a more intensive penetration of a market can be better achieved by *increasing* exports or by establishing a foreign manufacturing subsidiary. Thus the decision several years ago by Japanese television set producers to establish American plants after the U.S. government imposed "voluntary" export quotas on them was not designed to displace Japanese exports to the American market, but rather to supplement them with American-made Japanese goods. By barring *additional* imports, the quotas left those Japanese producers who wished to expand their sales in the American market with no other option.

By focusing attention on *costs* as the essential element in the export/investment decision, the effects of various developments can be systematically analyzed. The critical question about a particular development is whether it affects the cost of exporting or the cost of foreign investments. If it has no effect on either, it is not likely to influence the decision. If it increases the cost of the export option, it will tend to stimulate direct investment; if it increases the cost of direct investment, it will thereby stimulate exports. Similarly, anything that reduces the cost of one option will tend to bring about a shift toward use of that option and away from use of the other. In general, then, a change up or down in the cost of either of the two options—exports or direct investments—tends to make the companies' choice of the *other* option move in the same direction. Using this framework, we shall examine the impact of trade barriers, exchange rates, government regulations and tax laws on the investment/export decision.

Trade Restrictions and the Investment/Export Decision

Tariffs and nontariff trade barriers increase the costs associated with exporting to the protected market and hence tend to stimulate FDI. In extreme cases, trade obstacles can make the cost of exporting prohibitive; there may be no way foreign producers can legally and effectively penetrate a market protected by highly restrictive quotas. Faced with an obstacle of this nature, a firm's effective choice may be either to establish a manufacturing base within the foreign market or to give up on it completely. It is argued in Chapter 5 that the present drive to restrict FDIs in the United States is fueled, in large degree, by protectionist sentiment. It is not without irony to note, therefore, that past successful efforts to protect American manufacturers from the competition of imports are themselves one of the major factors responsible for these investments.

It is not difficult to provide illustrations of the impact of trade barriers on the export/investment decision. American direct investments in the European Economic Community increased by $9 billion during the 1960s. This represented a fourfold increase in the American investment position in the EEC. A major reason for this was the provision in the Treaty of Rome, which established the Community in 1958, calling for an initial reduction in, and an ultimate abolition of, tariffs on *intra*-Community trade in manufactured goods while maintaining common external tariffs on goods originating outside the Community. This obviously provided American firms with a powerful incentive to establish branches in one or another of the Community countries, which together constitute the richest market in the world except for the United States itself. By setting up a manufacturing plant in France, for example, an American firm could position itself to sell its products free of tariffs not only in the host country but in the markets of the other Community members as well.

High American tariffs on goods originating in Europe provide comparable incentives to European firms interested in penetrating American markets. This is a major reason why foreign firms account for a relatively large share of the output of the American chemical industry. An important contributing factor was a unique provision of the U.S. tariff law, only recently rescinded, applicable to certain chemicals only, called the American selling price formula—whose thinly disguised effect was to impose an exceptionally high tariff on this category of imports. One result, which the sponsors surely did not intend, was to provide foreign firms with strong incentives to establish manufacturing plants in the United States.

Exchange Rates and the Investment/Export Decision

Currency exchange rates can also exert a potent impact on company decisions whether to take the export route or the direct investment route. To understand why this is so, it is necessary to consider how exchange rates affect buying and selling between countries.

Suppose an English bicycle is priced to sell at £20. The *dollar* price of this bicycle to an American importer will depend on the dollar-pound exchange rate. At a rate of $2 = £1, the *dollar* price of the bicycle would be $40. At the rate of $4 = £1, the dollar price would be $80. It is apparent that at a given pound price, British bicycles would be more attractive to Americans when the pound is cheap in terms of dollars (£1 = $2) than when it is expensive (£1 = $4). It should be equally apparent that American exports will be more attractive to British customers the higher the price of the pound is in terms of the dollar. Thus an American product priced to sell at $30 would cost the British £15 at an exchange rate of $2 = £1, but only £7.50 at an exchange rate of $4 = £1.

The assumption that domestic prices remain constant when the exchange rate varies is, of course, highly unrealistic. Indeed, it is almost certain that a devaluation of the dollar from a rate of $2 = £1 to one of $4 = £1 will induce a rise in American prices and a decline in British prices. In the long run, it is not inconceivable, and under certain conditions it is inevitable, that the induced changes in domestic prices will completely offset the effects of the devaluation. In terms of our example, the domestic price of American goods could eventually rise from $30 to $60 when the value of the dollar is reduced by 50 percent against the pound, leaving the cost of American goods to the British importers the same after the devaluation as it was before.

During the transition period, however, before domestic prices have had time to adjust to the new exchange rate, a *disequilibrium* between domestic prices and exchange rates can emerge. And it is during this period that the exchange rate level can affect the export/investment decision. By increasing the cost of British exports to Americans, the now undervalued dollar provides British producers with an incentive to establish subsidiaries in the United States rather than to attempt to expand sales in the American markets through exports. At the same time, the undervalued dollar (or, what is the same thing, the overvalued pound) reduces the cost of American goods to the British, thereby increasing the attractiveness of the export option for those American producers who wish to expand their sales to the British market.

For a variety of reasons which cannot be explored here, the U.S. dollar was overvalued in the 1960s. This provided a fillip—two fillips, in fact—for the expansion of American direct investments abroad. First, it increased the foreign prices of American goods, making it more difficult for American firms to export. Second, it enabled American firms to acquire foreign assets at bargain prices.

More recently, the shoe has been on the other foot. Over the past few years, the dollar has depreciated against a number of currencies including the British pound, the German mark, the Swiss franc, the Dutch guilder and, until very recently, the Japanese yen. By making it more difficult for foreign firms to export their goods to the United States—that is, by increasing the cost of exporting—the undervalued dollar provided them with an incentive to establish foreign subsidiaries; and the value of foreign investments in the United States has increased substantially during this period (see Chapter 3). Significantly, Volkswagen officials cited the devaluation of the dollar against the deutsche mark as the major factor in their decision to establish manufacturing facilities in this country.

Government Regulations and the Investment/Export Decision

By altering the costs of exporting and investment, government regulations can, often inadvertently, affect the volume and the direction of FDIs. Three examples will suffice to show the important role government regulations can play in the investment/export decision.

During the 1960s, the United States suffered from balance-of-payments deficits which the government attempted to correct by imposing capital controls. The first step was the enactment of an "interest equalization tax" designed to reduce the after-tax earnings on foreign securities. This was followed by a "voluntary credit restraint program" which aimed to discourage foreign lending, particularly by American banks. In 1968, these restraints were made mandatory.

The effects of these measures on American *direct* investments abroad were dramatic. U.S. affiliates operating in Europe, prevented from borrowing from American banks, began to borrow locally. Rather than lose this lucrative international business, American banks established European subsidiaries. The impressive growth of American banking in Europe was thus due, in no small part, to the U.S. government's effort to constrain the "exports" of American banks.

A second example of how government regulations can impact on the investment decision is provided by the Federal Drug Administration. The FDA has ruled that new drugs cannot be sold in the American market until they have been satisfactorily tested. Foreign companies have learned from long experience that this requirement could be satisfied at substantially lower costs if their drugs were produced, as well as tested, in the United States instead of at home. This induced them to establish American branches which provided them with a base, in the absence of which they would have had little prospect of penetrating the American market.

Our third example shows how some government regulations can discourage FDIs. As was already noted, the expansion of foreign investments in the United States since 1972 has generated a good deal of anxiety. An early manifestation of this was the enactment by Congress of the Foreign Investment Study Act of 1974, which directed the Commerce and Treasury Departments to collect information on foreign investments in the United States. In 1977, the Department of Energy Organization Act required a comprehensive review of foreign investments in domestic energy industries. Finally, the Agricultural Foreign Investment Disclosure Act of 1978 required all foreign purchasers of U.S. agricultural land to register with the Federal government.

While the intent of these acts was largely informational, their implementation clearly has a negative effect on foreign investors. This is due not only to the substantial additional costs of complying with these acts—it has been estimated, for example, that foreign investors collectively would have to spend 131,000 man-hours to fill out the various forms—but also to foreign investors' fears that the confidential information would be made public, exposing them to additional costs and risks. One respondent added a pathetic appeal to his forms. He wrote: "Managers and stockholders requested that business letters [from the American government] not be sent to foreign address for fear of reprisal of kidnapping their children if property ownership in the United States is known."

The State Department has expressed concern about the possible adverse effects of collecting and publicizing information on foreign investments in the United States. Deputy Assistant Secretary Meissner, the department spokesman testifying before the House Committee on Foreign Affairs on this issue in 1979, drew a sharp distinction between collecting data to ensure that "policy-makers are able to react to changing trends in direct investment, and using public disclosure of data as a basis for discriminating against foreign investors." He also warned that a mandatory registration of foreign investments, a requirement of the Agricultural Foreign Investment Survey Act of 1978, can "easily become a regulatory screening mechanism for certan types of investments" and could "actively discourage foreign investors from operating in this country."

Tax Laws and the Investment/Export Decision

The Federal government's official policy is, as we have already noted, neither to encourage nor discourage FDI. Yet American tax laws depart from this policy in a way that has contributed to the out-migration of American firms. American corporations with profits above a certain level are subject to a 48 percent corporate income tax. To avoid discrimination against companies with foreign subsidiaries, the tax law provides a credit for taxes paid abroad. Thus an American corporation with an affiliate in Munich would have to pay the Internal Revenue Service only 23 percent on its foreign earnings *if* these earnings were subject to a 25 percent corporate income tax in Germany. The combined tax rate paid by this corporation would thus be equal to that paid by another corporation operating exclusively in the United States. In this regard, the impact of the American tax system is, to be sure, nondiscriminatory.

There is, however, another provision of the American tax law that discriminates in favor of U.S. investors abroad. The foreign earnings of American corporations are taxed by the U.S. government *only if they are repatriated.* By retaining their earnings abroad, American corporations can avoid paying taxes on a portion of their profits. This provision discriminates in their favor even if it is assumed that ultimately all foreign earnings will be repatriated and taxed. During the period these earnings are kept abroad, the corporations are in effect receiving from the government interest-free loans. At the current high levels of interest, this could have an important impact on the investment/export decision.

There are more blatant examples of tax laws affecting the volume and direction of investment flows. Many firms which are owned and controlled by principals elsewhere—some of which, in turn, have major investment positions in the United States—are officially headquartered in certain small countries such as the Netherlands Antilles, Panama or Bermuda, whose extraordinarily liberal tax laws have transformed them into tax havens for foreign corporations. By establishing headquarters offices in these countries, corporations from all over the world have been able to reduce their tax burdens.

Finally, a number of American states and cities, particularly those suffering from higher than average unemployment, have attempted to lure foreign enterprises by offering them, among other things, tax concessions. Since state and city taxes are usually a relatively small component of costs, however, there is some question as to whether these concessions have been effective in influencing foreign firms' decisions to establish American subsidiaries. It is highly likely that the major role they play is in influencing a foreign firm's decision as to where to locate its plant after it has already decided, on other grounds, to establish an American base.

The Investment/Export Decision: Summary

This review of the major factors that can influence a firm's choice between its two alternatives, exporting or investing abroad, while not comprehensive, suggests the basic forces at work. A firm intent on penetrating a major foreign market carefully compares the costs of achieving its objective by exporting with the costs of doing so by establishing a foreign subsidiary. It will tend to choose that route which minimizes its costs. We have shown that trade barriers, overvalued and undervalued exchange rates, government regulations and tax laws, singly and in combination, enter importantly in this calculus and hence affect both the direction and level of direct investment.

The significant role of government policy in influencing the foreign investment decision should not pass unnoticed. A government that wishes, for one reason or another, to reduce the volume of FDI within its jurisdiction, can do so without resort to outright restriction. Indeed, this objective can be achieved by lowering its trade barriers, adopting a more realistic exchange rate, eliminating those regulations that advertently or inadvertently increase the difficulties foreign firms experience in exporting goods and services to its market, and reforming its tax system to eliminate those provisions which encourage FDIs. By the same token, however, if a government adopts policies that restrict imports into its market and/or reduce the cost of establishing subsidiaries within its market, these policies will inevitably provide foreign firms with additional incentives to choose the investment option.

Investments in the Absence of the Export Option

While the investment/export calculus which we have emphasized thus far explains much of the foreign investment that multinational enterprises undertake in order to penetrate the more advanced countries' markets, it does not explain all. There are situations where firms do not have an export option at all, and have no means of selling abroad except through FDI. For example, their products may not be exportable; or they may have lost their comparative advantage and can no longer compete in the foreign market with exports. These firms may nevertheless decide to establish foreign subsidiaries because they believe their capital could earn a higher rate of return abroad than at home. In other cases, the decision to go abroad is made as part of a total strategy and not necessarily as a result of a careful appraisal of the export/investment question.

The absence of an export option is characteristic of many service industries. Foreign firms intent on competing in the American supermarket, department store, hotel and restaurant industries, to cite but a few examples, have no alternative but to invest directly in American outlets. The acquisition by foreign firms of Korvettes, A & P and the Grand Union supermarkets are well-known examples. Similarly, many foreign banks were initially attracted to the American market to service the U.S. affiliates of their domestic clients. A failure to establish American offices would inevitably have led to the loss of their business.

There are other situations where direct investment is the only feasible alternative for foreign firms, not because their products are incapable of being exported, but rather because they have already exhausted the export option and have lost—or are about to lose—their comparative advantage. This consideration played a critical role in the development of the celebrated product-cycle hypothesis by Harvard economist Raymond Vernon. According to Vernon, the establishment of foreign subsidiaries is the culmination of a long process which begins with decisions to spend large sums of money to invent and develop new products. The development of a product with some new and desirable characteristic confers on the innovating firm a valuable but temporary monopoly. This may be due to the protection offered by patents or, more commonly, to the innovating firm's exclusive possession of the knowledge required to produce the commodity.

The innovating firm exploits its monopolistic position, and amortizes its investment in research and development by selling its product in both the domestic and export markets.

With the passage of time, however, the innovator's monopoly begins to erode, and with it the source of its comparative advantage. Patent rights expire, the production process becomes standardized and the technology becomes widely known. Imitators, at home and abroad, are waiting in the wings to make their entry. To protect its now threatened share of the foreign market, in which its exports no longer enjoy a comparative advantage, the innovating firm decides to compete by manufacturing and marketing its product abroad. The decision to establish foreign subsidiaries is thus made after the export option has been exhausted. This hypothesis not only helps to explain part of the growth of FDI; it also provides some insight into why large and innovating firms are heavily represented among those with foreign affiliates.

Investment as a Component of Total Strategy

Finally, for some firms the decision to "go abroad" is more a reflection of a broad strategy than the outcome of a careful calculation of the costs of exporting and investing. Firms operating in oligopolistic markets frequently lose a degree of freedom; they are often forced to react to their competitors' actions. Thus, if one firm increases its advertising budget, or changes its product line, the others may feel compelled to follow suit out of fear that they will lose part of their market if they do not. Similarly, an oligopolistic firm whose market is worldwide may decide to establish operating affiliates abroad to neutralize the presence of its competitors. While it is difficult to cite concrete examples illustrating this, it is not unlikely that the expansion of foreign banking in the United States in recent years was, at least in part, a response to the previous invasion of Europe by American banks.

FDIs are also sometimes undertaken as part of a diversification strategy to insure against political risks. Companies operating in politically unstable countries may, for example, wish to establish American bases to ensure their continued existence should their home governments be replaced by administrations hostile to the business community. It has been reported that some French and Italian firms which established American affiliates in the late 1970s did so because they feared that the Communist parties in their countries would win electoral victories. There is little hard evidence to support this explanation, although it is known that some "refugee" capital from France and Italy took the form of portfolio investment in the United States and has for the most part since been repatriated.

Costs and Benefits to Host Countries

To some people, any level of FDI is too high. These people suffer from a not uncommon ailment, xenophobia, the fear of foreigners. As is the case with most phobias, the roots of this ailment lie deeply buried in the past, and for many who suffer from it there is no known cure. Sometimes, however, exposure to the feared object is helpful. Professor Jack Behrman of the University of North Carolina found that while foreign firms were generally disliked by some, the longer the firm was established, the less disliked and feared it was. Exposure transformed these people's illness from a general aversion to all foreigners to a dislike and fear of new ones.

Xenophobia is unquestionably responsible for part of the adverse reaction which almost invariably accompanies an increase in FDI. It cannot, however, be responsible for all of it. When someone of Senator William Proxmire's stature calls for a moratorium on foreign acquisition of American banks, his views cannot be cavalierly dismissed as an expression of an irrational fear. To Proxmire and others who agree with him, the growth of foreign banking and other foreign enterprises in the United States constitutes a clear and present danger. But what is this danger? Should the United States, in the interest of security and welfare, restrict such investments? These questions cannot be answered without considering the costs and benefits of FDIs to the host countries.

Although such cost-benefit calculations will vary greatly

depending on the nature of the investment and the circumstances of the host country, certain generalizations are possible. On the benefit side, host countries generally find that FDIs augment their resources and enable them to enjoy higher levels of capital formation than would otherwise be possible. These investments increase domestic output, provide additional employment opportunities and often result in an expansion of the host countries' exports. In addition, FDIs are a major conduit for the transfer of technology, managerial and other skills. Finally, they have a favorable impact on the host countries' economies by increasing competition, thereby lowering prices and increasing the availability of goods.

How real, or how decisive, these benefits are has been questioned by numerous critics, especially from the LDCs. Either the benefits themselves are more apparent than real, these critics say, or they are outweighed by the costs and risks. Among other things, they question the value to LDCs of the technology that is transferred in the investment process. In their view, this technology, which tends to be capital-intensive and employs relatively little labor, is appropriate to the resource endowments of the more advanced industrial countries, which have a scarcity of labor and an abundance of capital. The resource endowments of the LDCs, however, are fundamentally different. In these countries, not only is labor cheap but a large proportion of the labor force is permanently unemployed. The use of the advanced countries' technology in this radically different environment has little impact on development and exacerbates an already difficult social problem.

The value of the managerial and other skills that are transferred has also been questioned by LDC critics. The positions requiring these skills, it is alleged, are more often than not filled by expatriates. These skills, moreover, are of limited value to those who wish to leave the "modern" sector of the foreign investors to find employment in the indigenous sectors of the economy.

Some LDC critics also allege that MNCs take out more capital from the host countries than they bring in. Others charge that

MNCs injure the host country's trade or tax revenues through "transfer pricing." In this practice, when trade takes place among subsidiaries of the same parent company in different countries, the prices of goods and services exchanged by these subsidiaries are determined by the parent company in its own interests—typically to minimize taxes—and may vary substantially from going market prices to the disadvantage of the host country.

Although these arguments contain an important element of truth when applied to the LDCs, they are not nearly as relevant when the hosts are the more advanced industrial countries. Surely the technology transferred to the United States by European firms or to Europe by American firms will not be the wrong kind. It is highly unlikely that the skills acquired by those members of the local population who work for expatriate firms will be useless should they leave their positions to work for national firms. And transfer pricing is less likely to be a problem where the foreign enterprise is producing for the host country market rather than for export.

However, FDIs in Europe, the United States and other developed countries are often criticized on other grounds. To some, the problem is that the host countries will become so dependent on foreign technology that they will reduce their own research and development efforts. Others have expressed the fear that foreigners will gain control of "sensitive" industries—which are rarely precisely defined—thereby increasing the vulnerability of the host countries. Still others have argued that foreign ownership dilutes the home governments' ability to plan or regulate their economies, reducing the welfare of the host countries' citizens. French critics have argued, for example, that their government's attempts at economic planning were frustrated, if not sabotaged, by the American-owned corporations' alleged noncompliance with French regulations. In a similar vein, some Americans have argued that the failure to subject foreign banks to Federal Reserve regulations hampered the ability of the monetary authorities of the United States to regulate this country's economy.

Questions of Sovereignty

Up to this point the criticisms we have been reviewing have been on economic grounds only. However, noneconomic considerations also play an important role in the case against FDIs. Foreign enterprises are widely regarded, especially in LDCs, as a threat to the host countries' political integrity and sovereignty. The enormous financial resources at their disposal can be, and on occasion have been, used to bribe officials, to influence elections, to install governments favorable to the foreign investor, and to dispose of others regarded as hostile. Gunboat diplomacy, in the classic sense, may be a thing of the past; but the sensational disclosures concerning bribery and covert activities by American firms and the American government before and during Salvador Allende's presidency in Chile are still too recent, and too vividly remembered, to dismiss these concerns as paranoid delusions.

The fear that the host countries' sovereignty will be compromised is not confined to the LDCs, although in view of their history it is experienced most acutely there. Over the years a number of advanced industrial countries have complained that U.S. policies, as they affected American firms operating abroad, posed a challenge to their sovereignty. The problems arose mainly in two areas: The application of American antitrust law to American subsidiaries; and the American government's insistence that its regulations prohibiting the sale of "strategic" or military goods to proscribed countries are as applicable to subsidiaries as they are to domestic firms.

American antitrust policy differs in several fundamental respects from that of most other advanced industrial countries; industrial activities which are prohibited in the United States are not only permitted abroad but at times actively encouraged. The U.S. courts have ruled, however, that American subsidiaries abroad are subject to the antitrust laws to the degree that their behavior affects American commerce. This ruling—although somewhat softened by recent decisions—has resulted in the prosecution of a number of American firms for activities of their subsidiaries that were legal in the host countries. Such prosecutions, actual or threatened, have inhibited American subsidiaries from participating in host-government sponsored "rationalization" schemes calling for mergers, price-fixing agreements and other forms of interfirm cooperation which would cause them to run afoul of the American antitrust laws. It was experience of this kind that led a Canadian task force to assert that "any tendency for American-controlled firms in Canada to be reluctant to participate in Canadian rationalization programs because of American antitrust laws against mergers must be resisted by the Canadian authorities when such mergers are in the Canadian public interest as defined by Canadian law."

Various American laws and regulations prohibit the sale of goods classified as strategic or military to specified countries. The American government's position is that these regulations apply as fully to American subsidiaries operating abroad, and subject to the laws and policies of their respective host governments, as they do to domestic firms. This has led to some paradoxical results. The U.S. government prohibited IBM-France from selling computers to its host, the French government, because they were to be used in nuclear research and it was against American policy to sell "nuclear equipment" to any government which, like France, had not ratified the nuclear nonproliferation treaty of 1968. A South African-based American firm was ordered not to deliver vehicles to its host government because they could be converted to military use—the U.S. government having adhered to a United Nations Security Council resolution calling on member governments to prohibit the transfer of arms to South Africa. Numerous American affiliates in Western Europe were forbidden to sell "strategic" goods to Soviet-bloc countries, China and Cuba despite the fact that these prohibitions ran counter to the host countries' policies and were widely regarded as an infringement on their sovereignty.

This "infringement of sovereignty" issue was raised again in 1979 as a result of President Jimmy Carter's order to freeze Iran's dollar deposits in American banks following that country's seizure of the American embassy in Teheran. The U.S. government made it clear that the order applied to American banks operating abroad as well as at home. Japan and various

European governments protested on the grounds that banks operating under their jurisdiction were subject to their regulations, and that it was not in their national interest to freeze Iranian deposits.

It would be a mistake to exaggerate the importance of these conflicts. The infringements on the host countries' sovereignty were not central and for the most part it was possible to reach a satisfactory negotiated settlement. Yet an important principle is at stake. To appreciate the host government's dilemma, consider how the American government might react if ever Saudi Arabian authorities were to order a Saudi banking affiliate in the United States to impose sanctions on anyone engaged in business with Israel, or if a bank of Greek "parentage" received similar orders regarding Americans who do business with Turkey. Adherence to such an order would clearly bring the bank into conflict with American laws. Would the U.S. government, in these circumstances, be understanding and permit the foreign affiliate to violate U.S. laws and yet continue operations? Or would it cite the bank directors with civil or criminal contempt should they persist in the face of a court injunction to cease and desist? These are not unlike the difficult questions some host countries have had to face as a result of U.S. insistence that American subsidiaries are subject to its laws and regulations even where these conflict with the host governments' policies.

In general, most of the benefits the host countries derive from FDIs are quantifiable. Estimates can be made of the increase in the host countries' resources, production, employment and exports resulting from foreign investments. With greater difficulty, estimates can also be derived for the value of the skills and technology that are transferred—and even, perhaps, for the competitive stimulus and improved service to consumers that result. By the nature of the case, however, the costs incurred by the host countries are not measurable. How much, for example, is a slight loss of sovereignty worth? For this reason, it is difficult to strike a neat balance between the costs and benefits of direct investments. It is interesting to note, however, that despite a great deal of *Sturm und Drang,* few countries have banned FDIs. In fact, the vast majority, both developed and developing, have actively encouraged them. Is it not justifiable to conclude from this that these countries perceive these investments as beneficial?

This is not to suggest, of course, that either the MNCs or the host governments are satisfied with the *status quo*. For although these entities share a community of interest in some areas, there are others in which they come into conflict. The core of this conflict is easily identified. While conceding, at least by their actions, that on balance they have been benefited by FDIs, the host governments would like, where possible, to tilt the scales still further in their favor. Since success in this would inevitably reduce the rate of return on investments, the MNCs not only resist these efforts but, on occasion, even attempt to nullify some of the gains the host governments have already won. This jockeying for position can sometimes take on the appearance of a mortal conflict. One overwhelming consideration suggests, however, that it would be a mistake to view it in this way: The host government usually can force the MNC to vacate the premises. India's eviction of IBM—an action it has since regretted—is a case in point. This should be borne in mind when we consider in the next two chapters the alleged threat that FDIs pose for a powerful country like the United States.

3

Direct Investment: A Statistical Portrait

The major objective of this chapter is to draw a "statistical portrait" of the FDI position in the United States. As was already noted, the increase in this position in recent years has been a source of anxiety and has given rise to increased demands for a modification of the U.S. traditional open door policy. The purpose here is to shed some light on some of the more important questions that have come to the fore in the recent debate. Specifically, are foreigners "buying up" America, gaining control over sensitive industries, threatening American sovereignty and political integrity? The statistical portrait may not be able to answer all these questions conclusively. At the minimum, however, it will help dispel some of the myths that have developed.

The U.S. Investment Position Abroad

Before attention is turned to the foreign investment position in the United States, however, it is necessary to review briefly the American direct investment position abroad. The reasons for this are twofold. First, a concentration on the foreign investment position in the United States without some regard to the much larger American position abroad could lead to a serious distortion of perspective. At the extreme, it could create an erroneous impression that FDI is a one-way street and that the American economy is somehow being "exploited" by foreign investors. Second, and equally important, it is essential to remember that in matters of foreign investment as in matters of trade, reciprocity is a key word. If, for example, we want American-owned firms abroad to receive national treatment—that is, nondiscriminatory treatment by the host government—our success in this respect will be determined, at least in part, by the treatment we accord foreign investors in the United States. America's stake in its investments abroad should, therefore, be clearly understood in considering modifications in U.S. investment policies.

The value of the American direct investment position abroad exceeds that of any other country. It is estimated that the worldwide value of all countries' FDIs presently equals $300 billion. The United States accounts for approximately 55 percent of this amount. The post-World War II growth of American FDIs is shown in Table 1. Especially noteworthy is the rapid expansion of these investments since 1965. In the 15 years between 1950 and 1965 total American investments abroad

Table 1

The Foreign Direct Investment Position of the United States, 1950–78
(In billions of U.S. dollars)

Year	Value
1950	12
1960	32
1965	49
1970	75
1978	168

Source: Department of Commerce, *Survey of Current Business.*

increased by $37 billion: in the 13 years since 1965, a further increase of $119 billion occurred. Even after inflation is taken into account, the expansion has been impressive.

Which countries did American investors favor? In what industries did they invest? The answers are given in Table 2, from which a number of interesting facts emerge. First, U.S. firms abroad are heavily concentrated in the advanced industrial

Table 2

The Americ

U.S. Direct Investment Position
(In bil

	All Industries	Mining and Smelting	Petroleu
All countries	168.1	7.0	33.3
Developed countries	120.7	4.7	26.4
Canada	37.2	3.0	8.2
Europe	69.7	*	14.7
European Communities (9)	55.3	*	12.2
United Kingdom	20.3	*	5.9
West Germany	12.7	*	2.4
France	6.8	*	0.9
Switzerland	7.4	0	0.1
Japan	5.0	0	1.6
Australia, New Zealand	6.8	1.3[1]	1.0[1]
South Africa	2.0	[2]	[2]
Developing Countries	40.5	2.3	4.5
Latin American Republics	21.3	1.3	2.0
Other Western Hemisphere	11.2	0.4	1.7
Other Africa	3.4	0.5	2.1
Middle East	−2.1[3]	[2]	−3.5[3]
Other Asia and Pacific	6.7	[2]	2.3
International and unallocated	6.9	0	2.4

*Less than $50 million.
[1] Australia only; New Zealand figure not given. See note 2.
[2] Not given in source "to avoid disclosure of data of individual companies."
[3] Minus quantity means parent companies' net indebtedness to affiliates in this area exceeded their equitie
Figures may not add to exact totals because of rounding.
Source: U.S. Department of Commerce, *Survey of Current Business*, August 1979.

countries, which account for 72 percent of the $168 billion total. Within this group, the EEC countries with investments of $55 billion and Canada with investments of $37 billion were the most attractive targets. Of the $40 billion invested in the developing countries, Latin America with $32 billion accounted for 80 percent.

These investments were largely motivated by the investing

ke Abroad
eign Regions and Selected Countries, 1978
(llars)

anufacturing	Transport, Communications, Public Utilities	Trade	Finance, Insurance	Other
74.2	3.7	17.6	24.1	8.2
60.1	1.2	12.7	11.1	4.5
17.6	1.1	2.4	3.9	1.0
36.4	0.1	8.7	6.6	3.1
32.2	*	4.6	4.1	2.0
10.1	*	*	1.9	1.3
8.3	*	0.8	1.1	[2]
4.6	*	0.8	0.3	[2]
1.1	*	3.5	2.1	0.5
2.3	*	0.6	0.2	0.1
3.0	*	0.7	0.4[1]	0.2
0.7	*	0.2	*	0.1
14.1	0.6	4.2	11.1	3.5
10.9	[2]	2.7	2.7	[2]
0.8	[2]	0.4	7.6	[2]
0.3	0.1	0.2	0.1	0.2
0.2	*	0.1	0.2	[2]
2.0	0.2	1.0	0.6	[2]
0	1.8	0.7	1.9	0.1

firms' desire to sell goods and services in the host countries' markets. Department of Commerce data for 1976 show that sales to the host country markets by majority-owned affiliates of American companies accounted for 78 percent of all sales by affiliates operating in Canada, 73 percent in the EEC and 70 percent in Latin America.

Turning to the industrial composition of American direct investments abroad, the importance of the manufacturing sector is apparent. In the aggregate, this sector accounted for 44 percent of the total. In the advanced industrial countries, manufacturing accounted for 50 percent of the total, while it accounted for 35 percent in the developing countries. The investments in the manufacturing sector of the LDCs were motivated not only by the desire to expand sales in the host country markets, but also to produce labor-intensive goods for export to third-country markets.

The American position in trade, finance and insurance should also be noted. Overall, these sectors account for 25 percent of the total. The importance of American bank activities abroad appears not to have been fully appreciated by those currently clamoring for an increase in restrictions on foreign banking operations in the United States. Finally, in the light of the energy shortage, it should be noted that petroleum investments in both the developed and the developing countries account for 20 percent of the total American direct investment position abroad.

Ultimately, profitability determines the level of foreign investment. How are America's foreign direct investments faring? The Department of Commerce estimates that in 1978 these investments earned $26 billion. This represents an average rate of return of 16 percent. The repatriation of a portion of these earnings made a significant contribution to the U.S. balance of payments. It is estimated that in 1978 American firms operating abroad remitted $13 billion to their parent companies.

The importance of both these benefits of U.S. direct investment abroad—its contribution to the earnings of American enterprises and to the American balance of payments—should be borne in mind when the FDI position in the United States is examined.

The FDI Position in the United States

Against the backdrop of the American investment position abroad, the FDI position in the United States can now be examined. Its recent history is summarized in Table 3 and, in somewhat greater detail for the period 1973-78, in Table 4.

In absolute terms, the growth of foreign direct investments in the United States was quite modest until 1972. Between 1970 and 1978, however, these investments increased by $27.5 billion, a threefold rise. It is this steep increase, of course, that has given rise to the present concern. It is important, however, to view this development in proper balance. The *total* FDI position in the United States at year end 1978 was only equal to approximately 45 percent of the *increase* in the American direct investment position abroad between 1970 and 1978.

Who Are the Foreign Investors?

There is a widespread belief that members of the Organization of Petroleum Exporting Countries (OPEC) have used their expanded revenues since 1973 to acquire a large direct investment position. The facts, however, do not support this belief. At year end 1978, they accounted for less than 1 percent of the total investment.

As Table 5 reveals, real estate, rather than manufacturing, trade or finance, has been the most favored sector for such OPEC investment as has occurred. It accounts for 61 percent of the OPEC total, and for 22 percent of the $909 million of real estate investment money from all foreign sources. Anxiety on this subject has been accentuated by the fact that foreign real estate investments are almost certainly undervalued in official accounts, which include only the foreign investor's own funds. Since real estate investments are highly leveraged—that is, the investor typically borrows a high proportion of the purchase price from local sources—the value of the properties is much higher. Do OPEC real estate acquisitions include a significant proportion of America's farmland? A recent report by the Department of Agriculture—mandated by the Agricultural Foreign Investment Disclosure Act of 1978—provides the answer. At the present

Table 3

Foreign Direct Investments in the U.S.
(In billions of U.S. dollars)

Year	$
1950	3.3
1955	5.0
1960	6.9
1965	8.8
1970	13.3
1973	20.6
1975	27.7
1978	40.8

Source: U.S. Department of Commerce, *Survey of Current Business.*

Table 4

How Foreign Investment Grew in the U.S., 1973–78
(In billions of U.S. dollars)
By area or major country of origin, with manufacturing shown separately

	1973	1976	1978
All Areas	20.6	30.8	40.8
Manufacturing	*8.2*	*12.6*	*16.3*
Canada	4.2	5.9	6.2
Manufacturing	*2.3*	*3.4*	*3.3*
United Kingdom	5.4	5.8	7.4
Manufacturing	*1.6*	*2.0*	*2.9*
Europe excluding United Kingdom	8.5	14.4	20.6
Manufacturing	*3.2*	*5.5*	*8.0*
Japan	0.2	1.2	2.7
Manufacturing	*0.1*	*0.3*	*0.4*
Other	2.3	3.5	4.1
Manufacturing	*1.0*	*1.5*	*1.7*

Source: U.S. Department of Commerce, *Survey of Current Business,* August 1979.

Table 5

OPEC Members' Direct Investment Position in the United States, Year End 1978
(In millions of U.S. dollars)

Petroleum	4
Manufacturing	56
Trade	8
Finance	45
Insurance	3
Real Estate	199
Other	10
Total	325

Source: U.S. Department of Commerce, *Survey of Current Business*.

time *total* foreign holdings constitute less than one-half of one percent of American farmland. The department reported that in its judgment foreign ownership did not in any way constitute a problem for the United States. In passing, it should be noted that foreigners own 3 percent of all real estate in the United States. The greatest part of these holdings, however, is in the form of residential dwellings.

If the OPEC countries are not "buying up" America, who is? A striking fact about such buying up as has occurred is that the foreign parent companies involved are highly concentrated in a few countries (see Table 6); in 1978 eight countries accounted for nearly nine-tenths of the $41 billion total.

It should be noted that the Netherlands Antilles is on the list solely because it is the convenient "first foreign parent" of a number of U.S. affiliates whose "grandparent" and ultimate beneficiary company may be in, for example, the Netherlands or Switzerland. As already noted, a number of other small countries, especially Bermuda and Panama, are also widely used as "first parents." If the geographic origins of foreign investments were listed according to the homeland of the ultimate beneficiary, Table 6 would list only seven countries and these would probably account for a still larger share of the foreign investment total.

However one may feel about foreign ownership in general, it is difficult to escape the conclusion that the overwhelming majority of the foreign investment dollars in the United States are not from "hostile" countries. Indeed, the parent countries of 90 percent of the direct investments are those most closely allied to the United States. Even granting that some of these investments may belong to investors of other nationalities, it would be difficult to believe that these countries would try to use investment in the United States as a political Trojan horse.

Table 7 shows, in the aggregate and for each important "parent" investing country, the industry-by-industry distribution of FDI in the United States as of year end 1978. Predictably—since the desire to penetrate the rich American market is the primary factor motivating foreign investors—a large proportion of foreign direct investment is aimed at the local market. Thus investment in manufacturing, trade, finance and insurance

Table 6

Main Countries of Origin of Foreign Direct Investment in the United States in 1978

Country	Percent of total
Netherlands	24
United Kingdom	18
Canada	15
West Germany	8
Switzerland	7
Japan	7
France	5
Netherlands Antilles	5
Percent held by these countries	89

Source: U.S. Department of Commerce, *Survey of Current Business*, August 1979.

accounted for 75 percent of the total. The substantial foreign investment position in the petroleum industry—nearly 20 percent of the total—reflects the fact that petroleum is more an international than a national industry. Foreign oil companies have established subsidiaries in the United States for two basic reasons: to ensure that they receive their share of American crude oil; and to participate directly in the American market. Investment in the real estate industry, at $909 million, accounted for but 2 percent of the total.

The national origin of foreign investments in key industrial sectors gives further reassurance against political trouble. Canadian, Western European and Japanese investors accounted for 90 percent of the total in manufacturing, 94 percent in petroleum, 92 percent in trade, 88 percent in finance and insurance. By contrast, investors from these countries accounted for only 40 percent of the small (less than $1 billion) foreign investment in real estate. As for the members of OPEC, their unimportance in all the industrial sectors other than real estate is apparent.

The foregoing analysis, of course, assumes that incoming investment from an ally is unlikely to pose a political or strategic threat. Let us now for the sake of argument make a more pessimistic assumption: that a major investment position by *any* foreign nation or nations in a key U.S. industry would entail unacceptable risks to the national interest. On this assumption, it would be important to ask whether *any* foreigners have gained, or are on the verge of gaining, control of "sensitive" U.S. industries. To answer this question it is necessary to know the shares of American output attributable to foreign investment in the different sectors of the American economy. Fortunately, this information is available. As a consequence of the Foreign Investment Study Act of 1974, the Department of Commerce conducted a benchmark survey of FDIs in the United States as of that year. (Although the study was to be updated in a 1979 survey whose results are due for publication in 1981, it is unlikely that the new survey will show any major changes.)

As Table 8, based on the benchmark survey, shows, in 1974 all businesses in the United States produced goods and services

Table 7

The Forei[gn]

Foreign Direct Investm[ent]
(In bill[ions])

	All industries	Manufacturing Chemicals and allied products	Other manufa[c]turing
All countries	**40.8**	**5.6**	**10.7**
Canada	6.2	0.1	3.2
European Communities (9)	23.9	3.3	5.2
France	1.9	0.2	0.7
West Germany	3.2	1.1	0.4
Netherlands	9.8	0.8	2.0
United Kingdom	7.4	1.0	1.9
Other Europe	4.0	1.1	1.3
Japan	2.7	0.1	0.3
Australia, N. Z., S. Africa	0.1	*	0.1
Latin American Republics	0.6	0.2[1]	
Other Western Hemisphere	2.8	1.3[1]	
Middle East	0.3	*	*
Other Developing Countries	0.2	*	*
OPEC[2]	0.3	*	0.1

*Less than $50 million.
[1]Figure given is for all manufactures.
[2]OPEC membership includes countries included in geographic categories.
[3]Not given.
Figures may not add to exact totals because of rounding.
Source: U.S. Department of Commerce, *Survey of Current Business*, August 1979.

valued at $1,124 billion. Of this total, foreign affiliates in this country accounted for $24.7 billion or just over 2 percent. The affiliates' share varied significantly, however, from sector to sector. It did not exceed 3 percent in any of the following: manufacturing, transportation, communications and public utilities, wholesale trade, retail trade, or finance, insurance and real estate. On the other hand, it did account for 5 percent of the output in the mining industry and, officially, for 18 percent of total output in the petroleum industry. Actually, the percentage in the case of petroleum is exaggerated by a quirk in Commerce

ke in America
ition in the United States, 1978
(S. dollars)

etroleum	Trade	Finance	Insurance	Real Estate	All Other
7.9	**8.9**	**2.4**	**2.8**	**0.9**	**2.6**
0.8	0.9	0.2	0.3	0.1	0.7
6.5	5.1	1.2	1.8	0.2	0.9
0.2	0.5	0.2	*	*	*
*	1.4	0.2	0.1	*	*
5.1	0.7	0.5	0.2	*	0.5
0.5	2.2	0.1	1.4	0.1	0.2
0.1	0.8	0.2	0.4	*	0.1
[3]	1.4	0.6	[3]	*	0.1
[3]	0.1	−0.1	*	*	[3]
*	*	0.1	[3]	[3]	[3]
0.4	0.5	0.2	*	0.3	0.4
*	*	0.1	*	0.2	0.2
*	0.1	*	*	*	*
*	*	*	*	0.2	0.2

Department statistics, which excludes most transportation and marketing of oil and gas from the national petroleum figure, yet includes these oil-industry activities in the foreign figure. Still, even if we adjust for this anomaly, we find that the foreign affiliates' share of U.S. output in the petroleum industry is significant. Moreover, it is heavily concentrated in three companies: Shell (British and Dutch), Standard Oil of Ohio, or Sohio (British) and Petrofina (Belgian).

Should this relatively large foreign share in the vital U.S. oil industry be a source of concern? The Department of Energy does

Table 8

Production in America: The Foreign Affiliates' Share, 1974
Gross product of major industrial categories in the
United States in 1974, showing in each case the share
accounted for by foreign-controlled companies
(In billions of current dollars)

	1 Gross product of all U.S. business in this category	2 Gross product of foreign affiliates in this category	3 Col. 2 as % of Col. 1
All Industries	**1,123.6**	**24.7**	**2**
Mining	12.1	0.7	5
Petroleum	32.2	5.9	18
Manufacturing	323.1	11.1	3
Food and kindred products	31.0	2.2	7
Chemical and allied products	24.5	2.8	12
Primary metals	30.7	1.4	4
Transportation, communication, public utilities	121.5	0.7	0.5
Wholesale trade	110.6	3.0	3
Retail trade	132.8	1.2	1
Finance, insurance, real estate	116.7	1.5	1
Other	274.6	0.7	0.2

Source: U.S. Department of Commerce, *Survey of Current Business,* January 1979.

not believe so. In 1979, testifying before a House Subcommittee, Peter C. Borre, Deputy Assistant Secretary for International Energy Resources, observed that "one test of the significance of foreign ownership might be the behavior of those firms under stressed market conditions such as the Iranian oil supply interruption, or stringency. Although the parent companies of both Shell and Sohio were among those most severely affected by Iranian losses, we have seen no indication that their corporate decisions have been less favorable to the U.S. market than those of domestically based companies." Americans who have suffered through long gasoline lines would hardly regard such a cautious commendation as grounds for awarding these foreign affiliates a badge of merit; but it does suggest that sleep need not be lost over the mere fact that some of the gasoline in the U.S. market is being refined and distributed by companies owned abroad.

Petroleum aside, foreign affiliates produced a higher than average share of U.S. output in metallic mining, manufactured foods and chemicals and allied products. There are good economic reasons for this. In the chemical industry, for example, the parents of most of the foreign affiliates are in the United Kingdom, the Netherlands, Germany and Switzerland, countries with highly developed chemical technology. The transfer of this advanced technology to the affiliates has given them a competitive edge over American corporations. In addition, as we noted in the preceding chapter, the high American tariff on chemical products and the Federal Drug Administration's regulations on testing have made direct investment more attractive than exports for foreign chemical and pharmaceutical companies desiring to sell in the U.S. market. Finally, the deterrent effect of high U.S. wages does not operate in the capital-intensive, highly automated chemical industry as strongly as in labor-intensive industries.

The data do not lend support to the fear that foreigners have gained control of "sensitive" American industries. Foreign control of one-eighth of the U.S. chemical industry, or of one-sixth of the metallic mining in the United States—not involving any strategic metal—cannot be construed as a threat to any national interest. Still less can this be said of foreign control of 7 percent of the processed foods made in this country. For the most part, foreign participation in the U.S. economy remains modest. Even in those few sectors where foreign affiliates produce a higher than average share of total U.S. output, they do not represent any discernible strategic or political threat.

Table 9

U.S. Jobs and Compensation: The Foreign Affiliates' Share, 1974

Industry	Number of Employees (thousands) All firms in U.S.	Foreign affiliates	%	Compensation ($ billions) All firms in U.S.	Foreign affiliates	%	Compensation per employee ($ thousands) All firms in U.S.	Foreign affiliates
Mining	391	23	5.9	6	0.3	5.7	15.5	15.1
Petroleum	498	93	18.7	8	1.5	17.6	16.6	15.6
Manufacturing	19,300	551	2.9	245	6.7	2.7	12.7	12.1
Transportation, communications, public utilities	4,504	34	0.9	68	0.5	0.7	15.2	14.5
Wholesale trade	4,307	129	3.0	58	1.8	3.0	13.5	13.7
Retail trade	10,267	120	1.2	85	1.1	1.3	8.2	8.8
Finance, insurance, real estate	3,980	73	1.8	46	0.9	2.0	11.5	12.4
Other industries and services	17,073	57	0.3	173	0.5	0.3	10.1	8.7
TOTAL	60,320	1,079	1.8	690	13.2	1.9	11.4	12.2

Source: O.G. Whichard, "Employment and Employee Compensation of U.S. Affiliates of Foreign Companies," U.S. Department of Commerce, *Survey of Current Business*, December 1978.

The Balance-of-Payments Factor

A quite different kind of problem that is sometimes attributed to foreign investment is a drain on the U.S. balance of payments. How real is this? In 1978, foreigners earned approximately $4 billion on their direct investments in the United States. This represented a rate of return of 10.5 percent, substantially less than the rate earned by American investors abroad. Foreign corporate earnings amounted to $3.1 billion, of which $2.3 billion was reinvested and the balance remitted as dividends. If we assume that unincorporated affiliates remitted the same proportion of their earnings, we find the total impact of these foreign earnings on the American balance of payments was about $1 billion. It will be recalled that in 1978, American enterprises operating abroad remitted $13 billion. On direct investment accounts, therefore, the United States had a positive balance of $12 billion.

Investment from Abroad: Its Benefits

It is an economic truism that any well-placed, competently managed investment is likely to produce valuable results whether its source is domestic or foreign, next door or halfway around the world. Foreign investments in the United States are no exception. The benefits they provide for the American economy are not essentially different or foreign. They pay taxes into the U.S. Treasury. They provide stimulating competition—sometimes uncomfortable for competing domestic firms, but generally beneficial to the consumer in bringing better products at lower prices. Not infrequently they bring into the U.S. economy new technologies developed abroad. Finally, they provide well-paid jobs for American workers.

This matter of jobs deserves some comment at a time when unemployment in some U.S. industries remains a problem. The benchmark survey permits us to estimate the value of this benefit to the United States. Table 9 presents employment and employee compensation data for all U.S. businesses and for the foreign affiliates operating in the United States in 1974.

In that year foreign affiliates in the United States employed

1.1 million people—about 2 percent of employees in all U.S. businesses. Geographically, all regions of the country shared in this employment, and in percentages similar to their respective shares in the total U.S. work force: New England, 6; Middle Atlantic, 28; Great Lakes, 19; Plains, 4; Southeast, 21; Southwest, 6; Rocky Mountains, 2; Far West, 13; noncontinental U.S., 2.

Nationwide, the combined payroll of these firms came to $13 billion. Average compensation per employee was thus about $12,000—higher than the U.S. national average. This does not mean that foreign companies pay higher wages than their competitors, but simply that they are concentrated in relatively high-wage industries. In 1974, 51 percent of the people employed by foreign affiliates worked in manufacturing industries, 23 percent in wholesale and retail trade, 9 percent in petroleum, 2 percent in mining—and only 8 percent in the relatively low-paid service category, compared with over 13 percent for the nation as a whole.

Concluding Comment

We have completed our statistical portrait and evaluation of the FDI position in the United States. The above data clearly support the conclusion that foreign direct investment has been beneficial to the United States and does not pose any threat. However, we have yet to discuss these questions as they bear on what many regard as the most sensitive industry of all: banking. For that discussion we have reserved a separate chapter.

4

Banking: A Special Case

The central purpose of the banking system in a market economy is to act as a middleman between savers and investors. In performing this role, the bank has two primary obligations. The first is to ensure the safety of the funds entrusted to it by the depositors. The second is to satisfy the community's legitimate credit needs within the constraints of available resources. In the course of time, governments have found it necessary to regulate and supervise the banks, both to ensure that these obligations are appropriately discharged and to control the nation's money supply in the interest of national economic growth and stability.

The question of foreign ownership of banks has assumed importance because of a concern that foreign bankers will be insensitive to the host communities' needs and will complicate the host government's task of economic stabilization. For example, it has been argued—among others by New York State Superintendent of Banking Muriel Siebert—that foreign-owned banks may divert funds from local communities, depriving them of credit. Questions have also been raised as to whether foreign-owned banks can be regulated and supervised sufficiently to ensure both the safety of their deposits and their compliance with the monetary authorities' efforts to stabilize the economy. These concerns alone would justify singling out the banking industry for special consideration.

U.S. Bank Regulation

The uneven impact of government regulations on domestic and foreign banks was a key issue in the debate preceding the passage of the International Banking Act (IBA) of 1978. Although the details of this question are complex, the broad nature of the problem is not difficult to understand.

Banking is subject to a higher degree of regulation than most other industries, not just in the United States but in other countries as well. This regulation serves three purposes: to ensure that banks adhere to the laws of the jurisdictions under which they operate; to safeguard depositors' funds against undue risks by monitoring and auditing the banks' loan and investment activities; and to give the monetary authorities more effective control over the money supply in the interest of economic stabilization.

Although in other countries the regulation of banks is generally the responsibility of one authority, in the United States it is divided. The most important regulators in the United States are the various state banking commissions, the Federal Deposit Insurance Corporation (FDIC), the Board of Governors of the Federal Reserve System and the Comptroller of the Currency. Although state regulations are not uniform, they tend to be less stringent than those applied by the Federal regulatory agencies. The FDIC, which insures depositors against bank failures, for example, tends to be more conservative in its auditing and monitoring procedures than the state regulators. In addition, banks which belong to the Federal Reserve System are required to hold specified proportions of their demand deposit liabilities in Federal Reserve Banks. Since these reserves do not earn interest, member banks are, in effect, deprived of a rate of return on a portion of their assets.

All banks in the United States operate under either a state or a national charter. State banks are subject only to the less stringent

There is, however, an additional reason. As was already noted, the principle of national treatment—nondiscrimination between foreign and domestic enterprises—is the cornerstone of America's foreign investment policy. In a typical situation, a country formally adhering to this principle is frequently accused of violating it by discriminating against foreign firms. In the American banking industry, the reverse has occurred. Domestic

Many-Layered Thing

regulations of the states in which they are chartered—unless they choose to join the Federal Reserve System or the FDIC, in which case they also become subject to Federal regulation. Most state banks have elected to remain outside the Federal Reserve System but virtually all have joined the FDIC. Practically all state banks, therefore, are currently regulated by at least one Federal agency.

Banks operating under a national charter are required *to join both the FDIC and the Federal Reserve System. These banks are, therefore, subject to the more conservative auditing and monitoring procedures of the Federal regulators and must, in addition, tie up a proportion of their assets in nonincome-earning form. The national banks have long argued that this puts them at a competitive disadvantage* vis-à-vis *state banks, which can elect to remain outside the Federal Reserve System. At the present time there is a move to eliminate this inequity by requiring* all *banks to maintain noninterest-bearing reserves at the Federal Reserve Banks.*

Prior to the enactment of the IBA, foreign-owned banks in the United States did not qualify for national charters and thus could operate only under state charters; moreover, they were precluded by law from becoming members of either the Federal Reserve System or the FDIC. This state of affairs may have been disadvantageous in some ways; but its most notable effect was to put the foreign banks in a privileged position in that they were able to avoid both the more stringent auditing and monitoring procedures of the Federal authorities and the requirement that they hold some of their assets in non-income-earning reserves.

As is noted in the text, various provisions of the IBA have considerably narrowed the difference between foreign and domestic banks in regard to regulation.

banks have charged that American policies, regulations and procedures discriminate against them and in favor of foreign affiliates. Much of the recent controversy about foreign bank ownership revolves around this issue.

How Foreign Banks Grew

Foreign involvement in American banking has deep roots; some of the most venerable American banks had their origins abroad. It was not until recent years, however, that the foreign presence became significant. A number of factors combined to produce what has been called the "silent invasion."

1. The general growth of FDIs in the United States acted as a lure to foreign banks, which established U.S. offices to service the American affiliates of their domestic clients.

2. The acquisition of American banks in recent years was perceived by foreigners as a good investment. For a variety of reasons American bank stocks have been depressed, with many selling well below their book value. This, together with a depreciated dollar, has produced a situation where American banks could be purchased by foreigners at bargain prices.

3. The increase in the volume of dollars held abroad, the expansion of the Eurodollar markets, and the replacement of a fixed exchange rate system by a floating one have increased the value and importance of an American base from which these banks can participate directly in the important American money market, as well as in New York's expanding foreign exchange market.

4. Part of the increase in the foreign presence in the United States can be explained as a reflexive action to the expansion of American banking abroad. With the increased internationalization of economic activities, banking can no longer be regarded as a purely national industry. Foreign banks found it desirable to establish American bases simply to make up their loss of business to American banks which had invaded their home countries.

5. Finally, some banks established U.S. affiliates to compete directly for a share of the lucrative American banking market.

The increased foreign presence in the American banking

industry is apparent from the data. In 1972, American assets on deposit in 52 foreign banks operating in this country amounted to $24 billion. By year end 1978, 305 foreign banks held American deposits equal to $129 billion. In the latter year, foreign bank affiliates accounted for more than 13 percent of all commercial and industrial loans nationwide. In specific areas, the relative importance of foreign banks was even greater. In New York and California, where approximately 95 percent of affiliate assets are located, foreign banks in that year held 32 percent of all bank assets and accounted for 38 percent of all commercial loans.

This expansion in the foreign bank presence in the American market was accompanied by a significant diversification in these banks' activities. Not too long ago, foreign banks concentrated almost exclusively in the financing and "servicing" of international trade. In recent years, however, they have become more active in financing the general needs of foreign affiliates and even of some major U.S. corporations. It should be emphasized, however, that their activities are limited, for the most part, to the wholesale markets. With the exception of some British, Japanese and "ethnic" banks, foreign banks have avoided the retail market. By and large they have not been in competition with the small- and medium-sized regional and local banks which are the mainstay of the American banking system.

Is There a Threat?

The most dramatic complaints against foreign banks, however, are couched not in economic but in political terms. Judging from his comments to the various witnesses appearing before his Senate banking subcommittee, Senator H. John Heinz III, one of the leading advocates of a moratorium on foreign bank acquisitions, appears to be preoccupied with the possibility of American banks falling into "hostile" hands who will then use the banks to promote their nefarious interests. One scenario which he is fond of citing has the Palestinian Liberation Organization acquiring an American bank, directly or indirectly, and diverting the funds entrusted to it by depositors to finance Palestinian terrorism.

It is not without interest, therefore, to examine the ownership of foreign bank affiliates. In 1978, affiliates of European banks accounted for 49 percent of the foreign-owned standard bank assets in this country (commercial loans, money market assets, etc.); Japanese affiliates for 39 percent; affiliates of Canada and other countries, mainly Latin American and Australian, for the remainder. Table 10 lists the 19 biggest foreign-owned banks in the United States, identifying the parent and nationality of each.

These ownership data lay to rest, at least for the present, the fear that the "silent invasion" has resulted in hostile interests assuming an important position in the American banking industry. But they do not, *per se,* refute the often-heard argument that foreigners *can* use, indeed may have used, their American affiliates to divert funds abroad, thereby depriving the American community of needed credit and perhaps serving the kind of hostile purposes feared by Senator Heinz. Moreover, an examination of the consolidated balance sheet for foreign affiliates, published monthly by the Federal Reserve System, is not of much help in answering this question.

The best that can be done in this regard is to point out that if foreign ownership has resulted in an undesirable diversion of funds, it has eluded the attention of many careful and knowledgeable observers of the American banking scene. Thus in response to a congressional inquiry regarding his views about foreign acquisitions, John J. Duffy, executive vice-president of the Security Pacific National Bank, stated: "In general we have no objection to such acquisitions. To the extent that banks operate under the same Federal and state legal and regulatory constraints, we would not look upon the question of ownership as an important one. We are not aware that any problems have been identified as resulting from ownership of U.S. banks by foreign interests. We would presume that should any such difficulties become apparent, they would be dealt with at that time." A similar view was expressed by Paul A. Volcker, former president of the Federal Reserve Bank of New York and presently chairman of the Board of Governors of the Federal Reserve System: "[I]n my own observation institutions owned by reputa-

Table 10

The Biggest Foreign-Owned Banks[1]

U.S. Banking Corporation	Foreign Parent	Nationality
Marine Midland Bank	Hongkong & Shanghai Bank	Hong Kong
Union Bank (Ca.)	Standard Chartered Bank	United Kingdom
National Bank of N. America	National Westminster Bank	United Kingdom
Europ.-Amer. and Trust	European-American Group	Europe
California First Bank	Bank of Tokyo	Japan
Republic New York	Trade Development Bank	Luxembourg
Bank of Tokyo Trust (N.Y.)	Bank of Tokyo	Japan
Lloyds Bank California	Lloyds Bank	London
Bank Leumi Trust	Bank Leumi L'Israel	Israel
Sumitomo Bank of California	Sumitomo Bank	Japan
La Salle National Bank, Chicago	Algemene Bank Nederland	Netherlands
Barclays Bank of California	Barclays Bank	United Kingdom
Barclays Bank of N.Y.	Barclays Bank	United Kingdom
Golden State Sanwa Bank (Ca.)	Sanwa Bank	Japan
California Canadian Bank	Canadian Imperial Bank of Commerce	Canada
Chartered Bank of London (Ca.)	Standard Chartered Group	United Kingdom
Fuji Bank and Trust	Fuji Bank	Japan
Industrial Bank of Japan Trust	Industrial Bank of Japan	Japan
Schroder Bank and Trust (N.Y.)	Schroder Group	United Kingdom

[1] Banks with U.S. assets of over $200 million as of January 1, 1978.
Source: Federal Reserve Board.

ble foreign banks have in general displayed a sensitivity to the policies and requirements of U.S. authorities in their U.S. operations as close (and as appropriate) as that of purely U.S. institutions. Perhaps more importantly, banks in the United States are operating in a competitive market that provides discipline as well as opportunities for domestic and foreign-owned institutions alike. In this environment, neglect of service or credit needs of an area should rather quickly provide openings for other institutions." Similarly, Robert Carswell, deputy secretary of the Treasury, commented: "As of today [July 1979] there has been no suggestion that any significant past bank problem was the result of, or facilitated by, foreign ownership." Finally, Henry C. Wallich, a member of the Federal Reserve Board and the governor primarily responsible for overseeing foreign bank activities, has commented: "The record indicates that foreign-owned banking institutions are likely to live by the spirit as well as the letter of U.S. monetary policy measures.... This is not surprising since nonindigenous banks generally regard themselves as guests in the host country."

But what of the future? Might Senator Heinz' nightmare come to pass? In weighing this question, it is important to distinguish between possibilities and probabilities. Unquestionably, the *possibility* exists. However, those most closely responsible for the regulation of American banks almost uniformly agree that the probability is negligible. Before a foreign bank can establish an American affiliate it must convince the regulatory authorities that its proposals are in the best interest of the United States. To quote Federal Reserve Chairman Volcker again: "A fundamental prerequisite" for the establishment of an American affiliate "should be a wholehearted commitment to compliance with U.S. law, regulations and policy in its U.S. operations, a suitable degree of insulation of the operation of the U.S. subsidiary so that it can stand on its own feet, and responsiveness to informational requirements." Other experts, including Henry Wallich, have publicly stated that the American regulatory authorities already possess sufficient power to revoke the charter of any foreign affiliate whose activities are not in the broad interests of the United States. This is also clearly the position of John Duffy, whose views have already been cited.

The increase in the foreign banking presence has, however, created genuine problems, some but not all of which were resolved by the enactment of the International Banking Act (IBA) of 1978. The two major problems addressed by the act were that of national treatment and the degree of Federal regulation to which foreign banks should be subject. Before these issues are explored in detail, it is necessary to digress briefly to examine the structure of foreign banking in the United States as it existed before the passage of the IBA.

Four Kinds of Foreign Bank 'Presence'

Foreign banking in the United States assumes four institutional forms: subsidiaries, branches, agencies and representative offices. *Subsidiaries* are separate banks which are owned or controlled by foreign interests. They constitute a relatively unimportant component of foreign banking operations in the United States. As of December 1978 there were but 43 subsidiaries which collectively accounted for 20 percent of total foreign bank assets. With few exceptions, subsidiaries result from the acquisition by foreign interests of already existing domestic banks. Lloyds Bank of London, for example, established a subsidiary when it acquired First Western, an established California bank with an extensive network of branches.

In general, subsidiaries are not favored by foreign banks. The major reason for this is that subsidiaries are subject to American banking regulations which other forms of banking can avoid. In particular, subsidiaries are subject to the so-called 10 percent rule which limits the size of a loan to any one customer to 10 percent of the bank's capital. Since the American regulatory authorities have interpreted this rule to mean 10 percent of the subsidiary's capital, not 10 percent of the parent bank's capital, many foreign subsidiaries have been unable, because of low capitalization, to compete with American banks in the wholesale markets in which foreign banks in the United States specialize. For this reason, the subsidiaries have concentrated in the retail markets and in trust operations. Foreign banks rely on other institutional forms, branches and agencies for their wholesale banking and money market operations.

Foreign banks may establish *branches* in any state whose laws permit. Before the passage of the IBA, which made them eligible for Federal charters, foreign banks operated exclusively under state charters. State banking laws vary. Foreign banks are eligible to establish branches in New York, Illinois, California, Massachusetts, Pennsylvania, Oregon and Washington. Most foreign branches are located in New York, where they have been permitted to operate since 1961. Branching privileges are granted in New York to those foreign banks whose parent countries extend reciprocal treatment to New York residents. In Illinois, foreign branches are permitted in Chicago's loop area and then only if their parent countries extend reciprocity to Illinois residents. California permits branch banking, but before the enactment of the IBA it effectively prevented foreign banks from establishing branches there. This was due to a California requirement that all banks, including foreign ones, join the FDIC. Before the passage of the IBA, however, foreign banks were ineligible for membership. Pennsylvania's restrictions on foreign branch banking were so onerous that few foreign banks established branches in that state. Massachusetts, while permitting branch banking, has succeeded in attracting only two major foreign banks, Barclays and Bank Leumi L'Israel.

From the foreign bank's vantage point, branches have two major advantages over subsidiaries. In applying the 10 percent rule to branches, the base is the parent bank's total capital and not that of the branch alone. This permits a foreign branch to compete aggressively, and from all appearances, successfully, for the wholesale business of the large multinational enterprises. A second advantage is that it allows foreign banks to engage in interstate banking, a privilege which, as we shall see, is denied domestic banks.

The *agency* has been the most popular institutional form of foreign banking in the United States. Agency assets account for almost 50 percent of the total foreign assets in the U.S. banking industry. Unlike subsidiaries and branches, agencies may not accept deposits or engage in fiduciary operations (California represents the only exception to this restriction inasmuch as agencies located in that state are able to accept deposits from non-U.S. residents). For those foreign banks that wish to specialize in wholesale banking and that do not rely on deposits as a source of funding, the agency form has a number of distinct advantages. Among the more important of these are the relative freedom they enjoy from regulation and examination from state banking authorities—usually mandated to protect depositors—and the complete absence of limits on the size of loans that can be made to any one customer.

Unlike branches and subsidiaries, agencies do not engage in retail banking. They receive their funding from the parent bank and by borrowing on the Eurodollar markets. Their major activities include interbank lending in both the U.S. and the Eurodollar markets, investments in U.S. money markets, financing trade and foreign exchange market operations.

Many foreign banks maintain *representative offices* in the United States. These offices basically operate as agents for the parent bank. They neither receive deposits on their own account nor extend loans. Their major functions are to arrange loans from the parent bank to American-based clients, to receive checks from clients for transfer to the home office, to establish for the parent bank correspondent relationships with American banks and in general to provide whatever services they can to the parent bank or to the parent bank's American clients. Because Texas prohibits other forms of foreign banks, the representative office is particularly important there.

The Foreign Advantage

We can now turn to some peculiarities of U.S. banking laws and of the U.S. regulatory system which have created much difficulty in dealing with the phenomenon of foreign banks. As we shall see, many, but not all, of the difficulties were cleared up by enactment of the IBA. Before its passage, and to some degree even after, American banking laws and regulations had an uneven impact on domestic and foreign firms, resulting in discrimination in favor of the latter. This discriminatory treatment permitted foreigners to engage in activities forbidden to domestic banks and also permitted foreign affiliates to escape some regulatory procedures to which domestic banks were subject. Ironically, in this case it has been the domestic, not the foreign, banks that have clamored for application of the nondiscriminatory principle of "national treatment."

The domestic banks' case rests on four grounds. First, the McFadden Act of 1927 and the Douglas amendment to the Bank Holding Company Act of 1956 prohibit domestic banks from engaging in interstate banking—while foreign banks were left free (until the IBA) to establish branches in as many states as had laws permitting branch banks. Second, foreign banks were able to avoid many of the regulatory procedures and examinations to which domestic banks are subject because of their right to remain outside of both the Federal Reserve System and the FDIC. Third, while domestic commercial banks were prohibited by the Glass-Steagall Act of 1933 from engaging in investment banking activities and the securities business, foreign banks were permitted to establish commercial banks as well as investment banks and securities firms in the United States. Fourth, the combined effect of the antitrust laws' requirement that bank acquisition not result in a lessening of competition in local markets, and of the McFadden Act's ban on interstate banking, virtually precluded, and still precludes, the possibility of one American bank acquiring another. The result is to grant foreign banks a virtual monopoly on acquisitions.

This last point requires elucidation. Before a bank acquisition is approved by the appropriate U.S. regulatory authorities, a determination is made as to whether it would result in a lessening of competition. For all practical purposes, this would eliminate bids from any bank operating in the same area as the bank to be acquired. For example, a New York-based bank with the necessary resources to acquire the Marine Midland Bank would be almost automatically disqualified on the grounds that the takeover would result in a lessening of competition in the New

York area. At the same time, a California bank would be disqualified by the McFadden Act ban on interstate branching. Insofar as acquisitions are concerned, American banks have been placed in a "Catch 22" situation.

These constraints do not apply to foreign banks, since they are not covered by the McFadden Act's restrictions on interstate banking. One consequence of this differential treatment is that an American bank on the verge of bankruptcy could be faced with but two options: to go under or to be acquired by a foreign bank. A somewhat belated realization of this curious dilemma led the senatorial sponsors of a moratorium on foreign takeovers to modify their bill to allow a waiver in those cases where a foreign acquisition is required to prevent an American bank from failing.

Although there is merit to the domestic banks' contention that prior to the enactment of the IBA they were treated less favorably than foreign banks, their case is somewhat overdrawn. Thus, while it is true that the McFadden Act prohibits interstate branching, the domestic banks are able, for limited purposes, to get around this legislation by establishing Edge Act corporations. Under the Edge Act (1917), a commercial bank may set up a corporation in any state other than the one in which it is chartered—or in the case of a national bank, in other than its "home" state—in order to engage in an *international* banking business. Through Edge Act corporations, large domestic banks are thus able to compete with foreign banks across state borders despite the restrictions imposed on them by the McFadden Act. It should be noted, however, that these corporations are explicitly prohibited from conducting banking business in the United States except when it is "incidental to or for the purpose of carrying out transactions in foreign countries."

Domestic banks have discovered other ways to mitigate the adverse effects of legal restrictions on their operations. One student of banking, Professor Frank Edwards of the Columbia University Business School, has summarized the situation as follows: "Large U.S. banks are already operating interstate through Edge Act subsidiaries. They also operate across the state lines through bank holding companies which own trust companies, factoring companies and consumer credit companies. About the only thing they can't do interstate is to take retail deposits, but foreign banks are not competing in that area anyway. In terms of securities activities, the big banks have been advancing the frontiers of law domestically by handling private placements for customers. In addition, they conduct a rather extensive securities business abroad. In London, for example, they operate as merchant banks doing a full-line investment banking business."

The International Banking Act of 1978

When all is said and done, however, there is an element of validity in the domestic banks' argument that they have suffered from a degree of discrimination relative to foreign banks operating in the United States. The IBA was designed to correct this problem. The act addresses itself to six major topics: the problem of interstate banking; the impact of the dual banking system—state and Federal—on the operations of domestic and foreign banks; the role of Edge Act corporations; deposit insurance; the relationship between the Federal Reserve System and foreign banks; and the regulation of the nonbanking activities of the foreign banks. It should be noted that the act applies only to activities subsequent to its passage. A "grandfather clause" exempts all *preexisting* activities from the provisions of the act. Thus banks with substantial interests in the United States prior to the passage of the act will be affected only with respect to a subsequent expansion of their operations. (See Table 11).

Interstate branching. To eliminate the advantages foreign banks had enjoyed with regard to interstate branching, the IBA provided that henceforth foreign bank branches operating outside their "home" states would be prohibited from accepting deposits except and insofar as they were related to the branch's international banking operations. In this respect, interstate branches of the foreign banks have been made similar to the Edge Act corporations. In another respect, however, the two remain quite different; for, despite a recent attempt by the Federal Reserve

Table 11

The 'Grandfathered' Banks

Foreign banks with deposits above $25 billion whose preexisting U.S. operations are exempt from the International Banking Act of 1978 (see text, page 64)

Deposits, 1977 ($ billion)	Name of Bank	Headquarters country	States in which operating	U.S. offices
52	Banque Nationale de Paris	France	Calif., Ill., N.Y.	8
47	Credit Lyonnais, Paris	France	Calif., Ill., N.Y.	3
44	Dresdner Bank, Frankfurt	FRG	Calif., Ill., N.Y.	3
37	Barclays Bank Ltd., London	UK	Calif., Ga., Ill., Mass., N.Y., Pa., Virgin Is.	87
34	Commerzbank, Düsseldorf	FRG	Ill., N.Y.	2
34	National Westminster Bank, Ltd., London	UK	Calif., Ill., N.Y.	3
34	Dai-Ichi Kangyo Bank Ltd., Tokyo	Japan	Calif., Ill., N.Y.	3
30	Sumitomo Bank Ltd., Osaka	Japan	Calif., Ill., Hawaii, N.Y., Wash.	61
30	Fuji Bank Ltd., Tokyo	Japan	Calif., Ill., N.Y.	4
29	Bayeresche Vereinsbank, Munich	FRG	Calif., Ill., N.Y.	3
29	Mitsubishi Bank Ltd., Tokyo	Japan	Calif., Ill., N.Y.	13
28	Sanwa Bank Ltd., Osaka	Japan	Calif., Ill., N.Y.	11
25	Algemene Bank Nederland, Amsterdam	Netherlands	Calif., Ga., Ill., N.Y., Penn.	6

Source: Federal Reserve Bank

System to broaden the scope of the Edge Act corporations' lending activities, they are still precluded from extending loans except to finance international transactions—while the interstate branches of foreign banks may continue to finance the general credit needs of their clients.

Federal charters. Before the enactment of the IBA, all branches and agencies of foreign banks were chartered by the states in which they operated. The IBA put these foreign banks on a par with domestic banks by giving them a choice between a state charter and a Federal charter. Since a Federal charter will subject the foreign affiliates to the more rigorous Federal government regulatory authority, it is highly unlikely that many foreign banks will opt for it. Nevertheless the right to do so could be important for some banks. At the present time, for example, Canadian and Mexican banks are ineligible for New York State charters to establish branches. This is due to the fact that New York State requires full reciprocity for its citizens in the applicant's home country before a charter will be issued—a requirement which neither Canada nor Mexico can satisfy. Before the passage of the IBA, Canadian and Mexican banks were thus precluded from establishing branches in New York State. These banks, however, can now establish New York branches under a Federal charter.

Edge Act corporations. Prior to the passage of the IBA, only banks with majority U.S. ownership were eligible to establish Edge Act corporations. By eliminating this requirement, the IBA gave foreign banks the right to establish their own Edge Act corporations. Although foreign banks can presently accomplish the purposes of Edge Act corporations in other ways—by establishing agencies, for example—this new right is not a meaningless one. Through Edge Act corporations foreign banks can now operate in states which formerly excluded them.

FDIC membership. For the first time, the IBA made foreign banks operating in the United States eligible for membership in the FDIC. Indeed, the act mandates FDIC membership for all foreign banks operating under a Federal charter as well as for those operating under state charter in states which require such membership. Since the purpose of deposit insurance is to protect the "retail" depositor, the act exempts those foreign banks which agree not to accept deposits of less than $100,000. This exemption does not apply, however, to banks operating in states which require *all* banks to be members, as is the case, for example, in California.

'Fed' supervision. In one of its most controversial provisions, the IBA gave the Federal Reserve System the authority to examine foreign bank branches and agencies and to require them to maintain noninterest-bearing reserves at the Federal Reserve Banks if the total worldwide assets of their parents exceed $1 billion. In the case of state-chartered foreign branches and agencies, the "Fed" must consult with the state banking authorities before imposing the reserve requirements. Foreign banks registered a strong protest against these reserve requirements on the ground that state-chartered domestic banks can avoid tying up interest-free balances at the Federal Reserve Banks by remaining outside the Federal Reserve System. In the foreign banks' view, to require all foreign branches to maintain balances at the Federal Reserve Banks violates the principle of national treatment.

Nonbanking activities. Finally, to eliminate the inequity resulting from the fact that foreign banks were able to engage in nonbanking activities that are prohibited to domestic banks, the IBA provided that foreign banks which maintain branches and agencies in the United States would henceforth be regarded as bank holding companies. As such, they become subject to the Bank Holding Company Act of 1936 which forbids them to acquire more than 5 percent of the shares of any company which is not a bank without a determination by the Federal Reserve System that the company in question is "so closely related to banking as to be a proper incident thereto." This provision will require "new" foreign banks—the grandfather clause applies here too—to choose between an American commercial banking position and an American investment banking position; they cannot have both.

In general, the International Banking Act of 1978 succeeded in eliminating most of the inequities of the previous situation. It is, in many respects, a remarkable piece of legislation. Its most glaring defect was its failure to put domestic banks on an equal footing with foreign banks regarding acquisitions. The basic problem here is that this inequity could be removed only through fundamental changes in U.S. banking laws and regulations which go well beyond the question of foreign involvement in the American banking industry. It was the persistence of this problem that led Senators Proxmire and Heinz, soon after the passage of the IBA, to propose a temporary moratorium on foreign takeovers of American banks.

A Game for High Stakes

Whoever is looking for a key to the politics of the American banking industry could do worse than to study the position of the major U.S. banks during the Senate hearings on this moratorium proposal. A parade of witnesses representing the largest banks in the United States voiced general opposition to the moratorium. Instead, they urged Congress to repeal the McFadden Act and the Douglas amendment so that, as they put it, domestic banks could compete on a more equal footing with the foreign banks. It was the small and medium-sized banks that provided the main support for the moratorium and, more broadly, for further restrictions on foreign banks.

On the surface, both positions were paradoxical. Even though the smaller banks are not particularly threatened by foreign banks—which tend to specialize in wholesale banking and in financing international trade—they assumed the burden of opposing them. And even though it is the larger American banks that are most exposed to this foreign competition, they almost uniformly urged against limiting further the activities of the foreign banks.

In some part, the big banks' seeming restraint can be laid to their extensive foreign interests and their concern that a restrictive move on this side of the ocean would invite retaliation against them abroad. More important, however, they are playing a political game for higher stakes, and in this game the expansion of foreign banking in the United States is a useful development. Well before it occurred, the large American banks had started a campaign to remove the ban on interstate banking imposed by the McFadden Act and the Douglas amendment. The expansion of foreign banking provided them with a new, ready-made argument. If foreign banks are able to engage in interstate banking, they urged, then surely the principle of national treatment requires that domestic banks be granted the same privilege. One is tempted to say that if foreign banks did not exist, the large American banks would have to invent them.

As for the smaller banks, their main objective is precisely the reverse—to maintain the protection of the McFadden Act and the Douglas amendment against the big banks. The moratorium proposal served their purpose, i.e., to deprive the big banks of a logical and politically attractive argument for McFadden-Douglas repeal.

This case is somewhat exceptional in the politics of foreign investment. The main struggle here is between two *domestic* interests, with foreign competition a secondary consideration for one side and even less than secondary for the other. Protectionist sentiment flourishes on the weaker (small bank) side of the struggle, but in this case the protection sought is against a powerful domestic adversary.

The Case Against Restriction

As matters turned out, the moratorium proposal did not prevail. And foreign banks maintain their advantage with respect to acquisitions. It would be a mistake, however, to try to remedy this problem by restricting further the expansion of foreign bank activities in the United States. Foreigners have been a source of sorely needed capital for this country's growth. They have played an important role in introducing into the American banking industry superior techniques and management and have, through the competition they offer, reduced the cost of bank services. They have been good corporate citizens and responsible guests. The entire community would unquestionably be the loser were the activities of the foreign banks to be further restricted.

Moreover, as we have seen, no persuasive case has yet been made that new restrictions are necessary or desirable because of a threat to U.S. diplomatic or security interests.

5

What Future for Open Investment?

The dramatic expansion of foreign direct investment positions, whether in the United States or abroad, is but one aspect of the increasing internationalization of economic activity in recent years. The increase in the value and volume of international trade, of the international migration of labor and of the integration of national economies in common markets and free trade associations are other manifestations of this trend. In the 15 years or so following the immediate reconstruction after World War II, from say between 1958 and 1972, this internationalization brought enormous benefits to the market economies of the industrial world. This period was characterized by the most rapid economic growth the world has ever experienced; and, what is perhaps more significant, the fruits of this growth were widely shared by both the developed and the developing countries. Despite occasional expressions of frustration with the problems arising from "interdependence," there was a general consensus, sometimes expressed and at other times tacit, that the internationalization of economic activity contributed importantly to these results.

The Liberal Consensus Shattered

The consensus was shattered by events since 1972. The breakdown of the international monetary system established in 1944 at Bretton Woods, followed by the successive shocks to the world economic system administered by OPEC, had a profound impact on the climate of opinion. The economic universe was no longer perceived as expanding, and international activities—whether involving trade in commodities or the movement of people and capital—were less and less regarded as engines of growth; indeed, they were viewed rather as threats to the domestic economy. The liberal economic philosophy which for the most part had prevailed in international economic relations during the period of economic expansion was increasingly challenged by neomercantilistic doctrines. In a nonexpanding universe, international economic relations were looked upon as a zero-sum game; foreigners could only gain at the expense of domestic welfare.

The retreat from liberalism is evident in many areas. Though nominally still committed to trade liberalization, the advanced industrial countries, including the United States, have become increasingly protectionist. This is evidenced in the large number of petitions seeking relief from tariff concessions under the provisions of the escape clause; in the increased demands for the imposition of retaliatory antidumping duties; in the increased use of "industrial policies" to offset the liberalizing effects of negotiated tariff reductions; in the imposition of "voluntary" export quotas on less-developed countries to limit the expansion of their exports of labor-intensive goods; in the increase of nontariff barriers even within the EEC, which was explicitly formed to remove trade obstacles.

Trade, moreover, is but one area affected by the emergence of neomercantilistic sentiment. During the 1960s, many advanced industrial countries lured foreign workers in order to reduce the severe labor shortage from which they suffered. They filled an important need and occupied essential positions which were not attractive to the affluent local citizenry. With the onset of the recession following the quadrupling of oil prices in 1973, the domestic attitude toward foreign workers changed drastically. They were no longer viewed as fulfilling an important social need. Instead they were looked upon as interlopers who deprived the indigenous population of jobs. West Germany solved its incipient unemployment problem by the simple expedient of expelling these workers. Nor is this an isolated case. The awakened concern in the United States over illegal immigrants from Mexico and the Caribbean republics is due in no small measure to the transition from an era of growth and prosperity to one of stagnation.

It is the same change in economic climate that has now affected American thinking about international investments. In a contractionist environment, the competitive threat that these investments pose to those interests most adversely affected by them looms larger. In demanding restrictions on foreign investments these interests are behaving no differently from those who urge higher trade barriers because of competition from imports.

The present situation in the automobile industry provides an instructive example of the factors determining attitudes toward foreign investments. The very large increase in automobile imports into the United States in recent years has had an adverse effect both on the profits of the American automobile manufacturers and on the workers employed by them. It is not surprising, therefore, that management and labor joined forces in demanding increased protection from foreign imports. That the interests of these two groups are not identical, however, is manifested by their divergent attitudes toward foreign investment. The United Auto Workers' union is primarily interested in maintaining employment opportunities for its members. It has therefore combined its demand for increased protection with a call for an expansion of foreign makers' manufacturing operations in this country. Again not surprisingly, the domestic producers have opposed this proposal. To complicate matters still further, the automobile dealers who sell both domestic and foreign models have come out in opposition to the demand for an increase in trade barriers but have supported the union's proposal for an increase in FDIs in the automobile industry. Each of these groups is advocating a policy which it thinks will best protect its interest.

The desire for protection is thus a major reason for the opposition to direct foreign investments in the United States. Protectionism, however, is basically a device to redistribute income. The protected groups enjoy an increase in income at the expense of the rest of society. It can be demonstrated, moreover, that usually the losses incurred by the losers exceed the gains to the winners. Thus, while restrictions on foreign investments will clearly benefit some groups, they will reduce the economic welfare of the American society.

But are there not valid noneconomic grounds for restricting FDIs? This question cannot be answered in the abstract. Much depends on the situation of the host country. Historically, many developing countries have suffered a great deal at the hands of foreign investors. Should some of these countries now decide to restrict FDIs, despite a dramatic change in the international economic environment which has reduced their vulnerability, they may have valid reasons for doing so. Special circumstances may even lead some advanced industrial countries to restrict FDIs. Consider, for example, the Canadian case. Because of Canada's proximity to the United States, American corporations have gained control over a large segment of its economy. At the present time, few responsible Canadians regard this as a political threat. But it is alleged that Canadians do, as a result, suffer from a severe identity crisis. Canada may very well come to the conclusion one day that it is prepared to sacrifice some economic benefits by restricting foreign investments in order to ease these alleged psychological tensions.

Investment Rules: an International Approach

It is difficult, however, to construct a sound noneconomic argument to rationalize the restriction of FDIs in the United States. The present level of these investments is still relatively low, while their contribution to American output and employment is not insubstantial. There is no evidence to suggest that they pose now, or will pose in the foreseeable future, any serious challenge to the sovereignty, political integrity, security or identity of the United States. Finally, the fact that many countries, both advanced and less developed, presently restrict FDIs in one way or another is no argument for the United States to follow suit. It is, however, a sound reason why the United States should continue its efforts, in conjunction with other countries, to bring about a harmonization of national policies in this area. Some success has already been achieved. In 1976 all members of the Organization for Economic Cooperation and Development, with the exception of Turkey, endorsed the Declaration on International Investment and Multinational Enterprises, which not only reaffirmed their commitment to an open investment policy and to the principle of national treatment but also set forth common standards of behavior for both MNCs and the governments concerned. Meanwhile, in the UN and other international bodies where South confronts North, efforts continue against much heavier odds, and no doubt on a longer time scale, to frame rules on this subject acceptable to all concerned.

Such efforts seem bound to continue, for their subject is a durable one. Responding to both market and nonmarket forces, firms have found it profitable to go abroad, and host countries have, by and large, found it beneficial to receive them. It seems unlikely that these proven benefits will soon disappear on either side. Indeed, it is highly probable that the internationalization of production, a process which has fascinated observers in recent years, will prove to be only in its infancy.

What remains uncertain is whether national governments, which often tend to respond politically to narrower domestic pressures, can cooperate to control the difficulties that inevitably attend this essentially constructive internationalization process. The course set by the United States in this regard will have a profound effect on the outcome.

Glossary

Acquisition: purchase of a controlling interest in an existing company by another. Many FDIs are carried out by acquisition rather than by establishing a new entity.

Affiliate: synonymous with subsidiary.

Balance of payments: a summary of the international transactions of a country over a given period of time, including commodity, service and capital flows and gold movements.

Benchmark: measurement of economic data in a specific time period that is used as a base for comparison with comparable data in later periods.

Direct investment: ownership of a controlling interest in an operating company.

EEC: European Economic Community.

Edge Act: An act of Congress (1917) which made it lawful for commercial banks to set up corporations in any state other than the one in which it was chartered—or, in the case of a national bank, in other than its "home" state—in order to engage in an international banking business.

Eurodollars: dollar deposits held outside the United States, mainly by banks (both American and European) located in Europe, which lend them to local or foreign banks or to commercial borrowers.

FDA: the U.S. Food and Drug Administration.

FDI: foreign direct investment. See direct investment below. In FDI, the controlling firm is headquartered in one country and its subsidiary in another.

FDIC: Federal Deposit Insurance Corporation, a U.S. government corporation established in 1933 to insure small bank deposits against loss.

Grandparent company: a company which indirectly but actually (beneficially) owns an operating affiliate abroad, although legal ownership is vested in a nonoperating "first foreign parent." In many cases the latter, owned directly by the grandparent, is located in a third country which offers special tax or other advantages.

Host country: in discussion of an FDI, the host country is that in which the direct investment is located.

IBA: the U.S. International Banking Act of 1978.

LDC: less-developed country.

MNC: multinational corporation—one that has direct investments in a country other than that in which it is headquartered.

NIC: newly industrializing country.

Nontariff barrier (NTB): a governmental barrier against imports, other than a tariff. The more common type of NTBs are import quotas, artificially inflated customs valuation, and burdensome health, safety or packaging regulations whose effect is to restrict the volume of imports, intentionally or not.

OPEC: Organization of Petroleum Exporting Countries.

Parent company: in an FDI, the controlling company is said to be the "parent" of the foreign subsidiary which it controls.

Tariff: a schedule of duties (taxes) imposed by a country on imported (and sometimes exported) goods, usually as a percentage of their calculated value.

Tax haven: a country whose lenient tax laws make it advantageous for foreign companies to incorporate nonoperating affiliates in them.

Talking It Over

A Note for Students and Discussion Groups

This pamphlet, like its predecessors in the HEADLINE Series, is published for every serious reader, specialized or not, who takes an interest in the subject. Many of our readers will be in classrooms, seminars or community discussion groups. Particularly with them in mind, we present below some discussion questions—suggested as a starting point only—and references for further reading.

Discussion Questions

The author discusses a number of causes and motivations behind the recent criticism of foreign investment in the United States. What are they? What are the recent trends in such investment? And how do these trends impinge on American interests and attitudes?

The author points out that U.S. direct investment abroad is still several times greater than FDI in this country, and expresses the view that curbs on such investment that might be appropriate for smaller countries are not appropriate for the United States. Do you agree or disagree with this view? Why?

In the author's view, the conditions that gave rise to a sharp increase in FDIs in the United States during the 1970s are similar to those that led to even larger U.S. investments abroad, especially in Europe, after the establishment of the Common Market. What were the conditions he refers to?

In what way do governmental barriers against imports (tariffs, quotas, etc.) influence business decisions on direct investment abroad? What other kinds of government policies also affect the flow of direct investment?

Some critics of an "open" U.S. foreign investment policy argue that this policy is not reciprocated abroad. Foreign firms operating in the United States, they point out, benefit from the relatively free market system prevailing in this country, whereas in many foreign countries all businesses, including American firms, are subject to close governmental regulation and guidance. Others argue that such differences between national practices are acceptable so long as each country treats foreign and domestic firms alike, in accordance with the principle of national treatment. Which view do you think is right, and why?

In what ways is the regulation of foreign investors in the U.S. banking industry different from that in other U.S. industries? In this case, who would benefit most from full application of the principle of national treatment?

As the author points out, the line in the legislative battle over foreign banking in the United States was drawn primarily between the large and small U.S. banks, the former opposing and the latter favoring a moratorium on foreign takeovers. Which side do you think was in the right, from the point of view of the U.S. national interest? Explain your reasons.

In his concluding chapter the author refers to international efforts to establish agreed principles for the treatment of FDI, including the principle of national treatment. In your opinion, should U.S. adherence to such principles depend on the adherence of others, or should this country observe them regardless of what others do?

READING REFERENCES

Barnet, Richard J. and Muller, Ronald E., *Global Reach: The Power of the Multinational Corporation*. New York, Simon and Shuster,

1975.

Crowe, Kenneth C., *America for Sale*. New York, Doubleday, 1980 (paperback).

Cutler, Lloyd N., "Global Interdependence and the Multinational Firm." HEADLINE Series 239. New York, Foreign Policy Association, April 1978.

Kindleberger, Charles P., *American Business Abroad: Six Lectures on Direct Investment*. New Haven, Yale University Press, 1969 (paperback).

———, "America in the World Economy." HEADLINE Series 237. New York, Foreign Policy Association, October 1977.

———, ed., *The International Corporation: A Symposium*. Cambridge, Mass., MIT Press, 1970.

Madden, Carl H., ed., *The Case for the Multinational Corporation*. New York, Praeger, 1976.

Moran, Theodore H., *Multinational Corporations and Their Politics of Dependence: Copper in Chile*. Princeton, N.J., Princeton University Press, 1975 (paperback).

Organization for Economic Cooperation and Development, *International Investment and Multinational Enterprises: Revised Edition 1979*. Can be obtained from: OECD Publications and Information Center, Suite 1207-RP, 1750 Pennsylvania Ave., N.W., Washington, D.C. 20006.

Sichel, Werner, ed., *The Economic Effects of Multinational Corporations*, Michigan Business Papers #61. Ann Arbor, Mich., University of Michigan, 1975 (paperback).

Vernon, Raymond, *Sovereignty at Bay: The Multinational Spread of U.S. Enterprises*. New York, Basic Books, 1971.

———, *Storm Over Multinationals: The Real Issues*. Cambridge, Mass., Harvard University Press, 1977.